A BIRDWATCHII

SOUTHER

MALCOLM PALMER
with illustrations by
JOHN BUSBY

ARLEQUIN

ISBN 1 900159 50 3

First published 1997
Revised edition 2001
Reprinted 2002

Arlequin Press, 26 Broomfield Road, Chelmsford, Essex CM1 1SW
Telephone: 01245 267771
© Malcolm Palmer

A catalogue record for this book is available.

CONTENTS

Introduction

Much has been written, in more than one language, about the fascinating and huge region of Southern Spain. To put the task of writing this slim guide into perspective requires only a glance at the atlas, when it will readily be seen that we are dealing with an area half the size of England! The precise demarcation of the region covered by this volume is one of its novelties. Little attention has been given in the past to the Murcian Community — at least so far as birding is concerned – and the whole eastern part of Andalucía has also been rather cursorily treated in the past, the Province of Jaen suffering particularly badly.

I have written a guide to the Province of Alicante (Birdwatching Guide to Eastern Spain — Arlequin Press) which lies immediately to the north of Murcia, and started questing further afield by investigating the latter, some years ago. More recently, I have been involved in taking a succession of tours around Andalucía and have developed a great interest in the avifauna of that ancient land.

To the west of the region covered here lies the great estuary of the Guadalquivir, the Coto Doñana, in fact, and so much has been written about this area and its immediate surroundings, that it has been decided to 'skimp' the part of Andalucía which lies to the west of the Guadalquivir in order to devote more precious space to the relatively little-known regions of the southeast.

It is a region steeped in history, of wonderful natural beauty, peopled by tough, independent folk with a fiery mixture of Moorish and Gypsy origins and lore. No visit to this sunny corner of Europe can confine itself entirely to the birds. The rest of the natural history is fascinating, but the culture and heritage, food and traditions, of what is perhaps the hottest part of Europe, combine to offer much more to the discerning traveller.

Another guide in this serious (Birdwatching Guide to Extremadura — Arlequin Press) covers the area to the northwest, but for the sake of completeness, a little corner of Castilla-La Mancha is mentioned, though strictly speaking, it is outside our region.

It is true to say that many guides of this type can be tediously repetitive with successions of 'sites', many of which produce much the same birds. Exciting though it may be to a Spanish ornithologist to find a Robin breeding in some mountain area the readers of this guide will be unlikely to find this interesting. For this reason, as well as to save space for more useful items of information, full lists of the birds you are likely to see at each site are omitted and only the more 'interesting' species rate a mention. This need not, however, simply be on grounds of rarity and factors such as the presence of huge flocks of a species may lead to its inclusion.

As with any guide of this type it will be out of date the moment it is written, the more so in such an arid part of the world, because water levels in many of the lagoons and other waters are crucial to the presence or otherwise of many species. In the case of mountains, such a vast area contains many ranges which, for reasons of inaccessibility or simply because it hasn't occurred to anyone to go there, have received inadequate coverage. Information regarding any omissions or other information, would be gratefully received.

Malcolm J. Palmer
Apartado 360
03130 Santa Pola
Alicante

South-east Spain
Area
Administratively, Spain is split into autonomous regions, or *Comunidades*, and we shall be dealing largely with two of these, the vast area of Andalucía, whose provinces, Almería, Granada, Jaén, Málaga, Cádiz, and part of Córdoba and Sevilla come within our scope, and the Province of Murcia, which forms a *Comunidad* all its own. These autonomous regions were set up on the death of General Franco in the seventies and are extremely unequal in areas covered. One can only conclude that nobody else wanted Murcia! Our area is bordered by the Mediterranean to the south and east, by the regions of Valencia and Castilla-la Mancha to the north and by the great river Guadalquivir's lower reaches to the west. In total, the area covered measures some 450 kilometres by 150, or some 70,000 square kilometres. It is, in fact, something like twice the size of Wales.

Geology
Geologically speaking, the vast majority of the region consists of 'alpine' fold mountains, often rugged in the highest areas and with frequently outcropping crystalline cores. Recent alluvial deposits occur here and there to complete the picture. The Andalucían mountains are sometimes referred to as the 'Baetic Cordillera', comprising the vast majority of the region.

Climate
Climatically, mountains predominate in the formation of weather here, but the region lies in what is almost certainly the most arid part of Europe and much of the province of Almería is officially classified as desert, with a rainfall in some areas as low as 12 centimetres per annum. The rain is of an extremely erratic and unpredictable nature varying wildly over much of the region. Much of Andalucía enjoys four or five virtually completely dry months each year. In the mountains, however, this can be markedly different and in the area to the north of Gibraltar the greenery testifies to a much higher annual rainfall (above 160 centimetres). Over the vast majority of the region the July average temperature exceeds 25 degrees celsius — the high mountains of the Sierra Nevada being the sole exception with a summer mean below 20 degrees. The coastal lowlands are pleasantly mild in winter with a mean of 10-15 degrees, but very cold conditions predominate in the high mountains where temperatures fall below freezing for several months.

It is worth reflecting here that the Sierra Nevada contains the highest mountains in mainland Spain, the peak of Mulhacen reaching almost 3,500 metres in altitude, and that a thriving ski resort exists nearby.

Vegetation
The region lies to the south of the southern limit, for example, of Beech trees, and the coastal region is within the zone of Date Palms and Orange trees alike. the mountains are covered, to a great extent, in *Esparto* grass and are areas beloved of botanists. Some of the Sierras contain endemic plants found nowhere else and African species also occur in some places.

Much cultivation has taken place in large tracts of the region and the plastic greenhouses covering much of Almería's coast are a dreadful sight. It may be worth realising that ahuge percentage of Iberia was once covered in evergreen oak forest of which only fragments now remain.

In many places terracing has been carried out on hillsides and occasional irrigation-reservoirs provide artificial habitat.

In Jaén Province vast areas are given over to olive cultivation, making for a sterile landscape with symmetrical rows of trees as far as the eye can see.

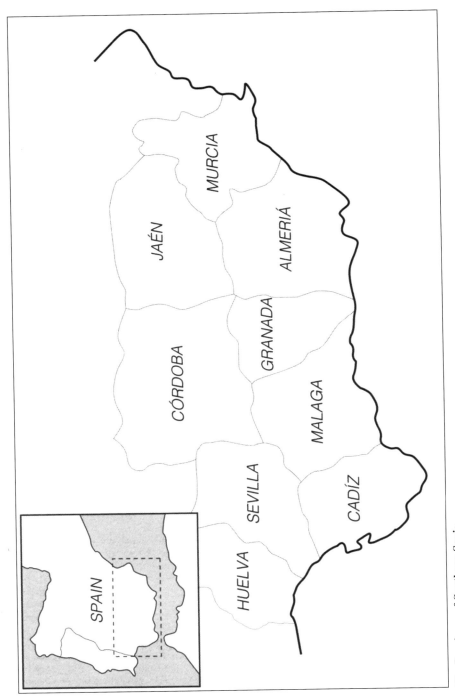

The Provinces of Southern Spain.

The same goes for the sherry-producing area around Jerez in the far west of our region, where the whitish soil and intensive cultivation necessary to the grapevines provides a boring vista.

Much more interesting are the parts where the rearing of fighting bulls is carried out. Here open woodland is the usual vegetation, with oaks the most numerous trees by far. Coastal pines can also be of great interest, but much of the coast throughout the region is given over to the Great God Tourism and there are few quiet beaches, especially in the summer season.

We have placed the birding sites in order of province, for ease of use, though administrative boundaries seem irrelevant, both to the birds (notoriously poor readers!) and to the birders, but we have tried to follow a logical sequence. The block-maps should be consulted as to the relative positions of the sites.

General Information
Travel to the region
Travel to the region presents few problems these days. It is a far cry from the days when I made my first expedition to this corner of Europe. Then you were obliged to drive all the way, often on indifferent roads, staying in even more indifferent hotels — or in my case, camping at primitive sites — and all the children of the town turned out to look at their very first foreigner.

Now, typically, you would fly to one of the main airports serving the region, perhaps hiring a car when you arrive, and stay in splendid modern hotels at very reasonable prices.

Charter services are to be found to Málaga and Alicante (just out of the region to the north, but well worth investigating for its cheap flights!) and, on a smaller scale, to Almería and Murcia (San Javier). There are some services to Sevilla and regular scheduled services, of course, to Madrid. If you wish to drive all the way it is worth bearing in mind that it is a very long way to drive! To drive across France is just about a hard day's work for anyone, then you need another day to drive across Spain — and that's if you step on it! Roads are good now, but you should remember: Motorway tolls — they mount up and the Euro doesn't help 'French prices are high'. Summertime — Roads can get very busy and driving is a hot, sticky, job. Ferry fares — these can be very high, especially in summer. If you are still determined to bring your car all the way it may be worth considering two options which would help. One is to catch one of the excellent ferry services that run from the south of England to the north of Spain (Portsmouth-Bilbao or Plymouth-Santander). Another would be the Motorail service on which you can cross France in comfort. All these options tend to be more expensive than flying, but if you have a long holiday and wish to treat the journey as a part of it, all well and good.

Travelling about
With the entry of Spain into the EC, a good deal of money became available for road-building and the result of this is that the roads throughout most of the region are first-class, though it is still perfectly possible to come across a stretch of many kilometres that will shake the teeth out of your head. This is particularly so in out-of-the-way provinces like Jaen, for example, and minor roads anywhere can be variable. The major motorways are almost invariably good, though they are usually only two-lane jobs which can be trying when busy.

Driving standards are also variable. Lorry drivers tend to be courteous and helpful, but this cannot be said for a great many car drivers who frequently exhibit signs of impatience and very often approach the car in front much too closely. Extreme caution should be exercised.

The rules of the road, widely ignored by many natives it seems, are WORTH OBEYING. Fines — on the spot — start at the equivalent of £60, and go up steeply for even the most trivial offences. If you are stopped, be courteous and apologetic and the Guardia Civil will be likewise. Bluster and you will find it reflected in the fine.

Things to avoid
Not wearing seatbelts.
Speeding — there are many radar traps and they use unmarked cars.
Crossing a white line — don't, ever.
Not observing a 'stop' sign — and they are often in what seem daft places.
Parking anywhere where there is a white line along the roadside.

Having said all of this driving in southeast Spain can be thoroughly enjoyable and you will usually meet few cars off the main roads — except of course when you park on a dodgy corner to have a squint at that soaring raptor, when you can guarantee that the 'Boys in Green' will show up within seconds.

Motoring is probably the only way to get the best out of such a vast area, but you can and should, of course, leave your car and walk whenever you are able. The rule then, as anywhere, is lock any 'goodies' out of sight in the boot or take them with you. Spain is neither more nor less lawless than other countries — it is a shame to risk spoiling your holiday.

Another system, of course, is to join an organised tour and there are several companies currently offering such visits, often with experienced local guides. One such is Calandra Holidays whose brochure you can obtain by calling 01223 872107.

Car hire can be negotiated at all major airports, but don't leave it until you get there or your options will be restricted to the international companies who charge a lot more than the local people. Calandra Holidays, again, can negotiate a favourable deal, at least at Alicante, and most flight companies will be pleased to offer car hire as a part of the deal.

When to go
It is always tempting to head for Mediterranean destinations in spring. The birds are newly-arrived, in good plumage, and in good variety. In southeast Spain you must gear it to what you wish to see and remember that spring is early. It is no good going in mid-May and expecting to see a lot of passage as the birds may well have gone through already. Likewise, it is no use going in early April and hoping for, for example, Roller and Red-necked Nightjar, which may well not have arrived. Other seasons too have their points and you will see a good range of birds in autumn or even in winter, when of course, you should be able to see some impressive flocks of wildfowl and the like. Perhaps the only time NOT to visit the region is in summer, when temperatures soar well into the high thirties. Birding is not a pleasant experience in that kind of heat. In conclusion, do your homework and decide on a time when you will have at least a decent chance of finding the particular species you wish to see.

Where to stay
Spanish hotels are much cheaper in general than their British equivalents and the system of inspection ensures that they are almost always spotlessly clean. The number of stars exhibited may affect the price more than it affects the standards of service, however, and one-star establishments may well prove adequate for all practical purposes, but it does depend on where you are. The rule, here as elsewhere, is to avoid staying in 'touristy' places if possible.

Camping is very easy in Spain, but again, avoid midsummer if you want to be sure of getting a pitch.

Food and drink
Andalucía is famed for its food and drink, and delicious local dishes can be a feature of

your holiday especially if you are prepared to be just a touch adventurous. Here the tradition of giving you tapas with any drink you order remains. The word simply means 'lid' and the tradition started when the bar-owner used to put a little plate on top of your drink to keep the flies off it, then added a little bite to eat — presumably to attract the flies back! Now you may well get just a little piece of ham speared to a bit of bread, or an anchovy, or slice of sausage.

Lunch tends to be the main meal of the day for most Andalucians and Murcians and is taken at about three o'clock. It can be huge! In the evening they will usually eat a much lighter meal, often after eleven. Breakfast sometimes consists of nothing more than a coffee and a cognac, but a snack may well be taken in mid-morning (*almuerzo*).

This sort of timetable is unlikely to appeal to most birders who will want a snack lunch — never a problem — a delicious sandwich (*bocadillo*) can be rustled up in almost any bar — then a major meal in the evening. Most hotels will oblige and there are usually restaurants around. In this connection, it may be worth knowing that restaurants in Spain are obliged to offer a relatively inexpensive inclusive meal on their menu. This is known as the *'menu del dia'*, or simply *'menu'*. However, this may well not be on offer in the evenings when you will be obliged to go *à la carte*. Andalucían food is very varied and includes the refreshing cold soup *gazpacho andaluz*, for which it is famous. Nearer the coast seafood predominates, whilst the interior of Murcia, for example, is famed for its cold meats and sausages. Cazorla is well known for its delicious trout and you can't go to Jaén Province without trying some of their famous olives. For the plain eater lamb chops are always full of flavour and for the more adventurous, the local snails (*caracoles*) in Murcia are a treat. The universally enjoyed drink is red wine, except in the sherry-producing areas of Cádiz Province where sherries are drunk at the slightest excuse, even with meals. Beer is also widely drunk and the indigenous 'Cruzcampo' and other brands are just right for the weather. You should, of course, bear in mind that drinking and driving is as frowned upon in Spain as anywhere and can lead to heavy fines and worse.

In hotels, breakfast will almost invariably be nothing more than a coffee and a bit of toast, which you can take in the British style with butter and jam, or as the locals do, with olive oil and salt.

It is as well to have a bottle of water with you in your car to avoid dehydration, especially in remoter areas.

People and customs

The people of Andalucía are about the least 'European' of all the people of that continent in that they are at least partly descended from North African stock. The 'reconquest' was relatively recent, Granada being last to fall at the end of the fifteenth century, and the Moorish tradition lives on in music as well as in architecture and the Spanish language. Add to this the fact that a huge gypsy contingent settled in Spain after migrating thousands of miles from the borders of India and you begin to realise the reason for the dark countenances — and the wild rhythms of *flamenco*. They are hospitable people with an inborn politeness but strong opinions. They have little reverence for Madrid and its politicians and will vociferously defend their traditions and values. Bullfighting is one tradition which arouses passions in foreigners and if you are opposed to it, it may be well to avoid the subject! You are on safe ground, however, with football and the local teams are well supported. The language spoken universally in Andalucía is *Castellano*, or classic Spanish, but it may be spoken with a very strong accent, a lot of s's being dropped from their proper place and the c's and z's will be pronounced as they are in South America (as sybillants), so even those with a grasp of Spanish may find initial problems throughout the region. Outside the main tourist centres few people speak English.

Shops tend to open in the mornings from nine o'clock until about two, then again in the evenings (not Saturday) from five to eightish. Banks are closed in the afternoons. National *fiestas* are always a chance for everywhere to close, as they will also do on local ones which are much less predictable. These latter can also transform a sleepy little town into a raving pandemonium with sleep out of the question at least until about five o'clock in the morning. At eight all the revellers will seem to be in the bars again!

In conclusion, Spain, and particularly the region covered by this guide, is about as un-European as you could find this side of the Mediterranean and it behoves any visitor to be ready for the shock. If they are, they will enjoy a region as diverse as it is beautiful, as hospitable as it is interesting.

Hazards

Mosquitoes spring instantly to mind under this heading but they are certainly no worse in Southern Spain than in almost any part of Europe and you need take no special precautions — at least no more than you might in Britain.

There is only one venomous snake in the region, Lataste's Viper. An irascible creature, it will bite readily if disturbed but is not very big and a bite would cause more in the way of shock than actual harm producing a nasty swelling and possibly a day in bed. It goes without saying, however, that you should seek medical assistance if bitten. The same goes for the small scorpions you may encounter (but only if you go looking for them under rocks!). Numerous wasps, hornets and horseflies can give nasty stings, but you are far more likely to fall foul of the cheap alcoholic beverages which should be approached with caution. Wine at a tiny fraction of the prices of other countries can lead to drastic over-consumption and it is my experience that most of what tourists put down to 'dodgy shellfish' actually stems from a lethal combination of wine and sunshine and consequent dehydration. Pickpockets operate in markets as widely as they do anywhere and the major cities are only slightly safer places than their British counterparts, Sevilla, in particular, has a reputation for street crimes. British registrations and obvious hire cars may well be conspicuous targets. I always advise people to remove the hire company's sticker as soon as they pick up the car.

You should read the small print on any travel insurance you contract and travellers from other EC countries should carry their form E111 in order to claim reciprocal medical cover whilst in Spain.

Maps, etc.

The Michelin maps, covering Spain in half-a-dozen big sheets, are perfectly adequate for route-finding, and it is worth updating any old ones you may have as motorways are always being completed. For more detailed maps of a particular area, for walking for instance, there are the Spanish military equivalent of Ordnance Survey maps which can be obtained in the UK, from Stanford's in Leicester Square. You may not normally find these if you wait until you arrive in Spain unless you plan to spend a day in a large city first. Guide books are plentiful but the majority seem more concerned with historical background than the sort of things you want to know!

Diversions

Not all birders wish to spend the whole holiday 'twitching' frantically hither and thither and there is much to enjoy besides. The Alhambra at Granada is one of the most-visited buildings in the world and deservedly so. Entrance fees are very reasonable and it would be a great shame to miss it. The rest of the city of Granada is worth a little time too, with many wonderful old buildings. The old Arab quarter of Albaicin is quite an experience.

Elsewhere there are cave-dwellings at Guadix, a scenic town in Cazoria and many beautiful villages throughout the region. You can sample the delights of beach resorts on the Costa del Sol and further east around Almería, ski in the Sierra Nevada, play golf at any number of places, enjoy the cliff-top town of Ronda, watch a bullfight if you so wish (almost anywhere in summer — you just have to be in a town when one happens), or make a detour into one of the great cities, Sevilla or Córdoba. The delights of these cities do not fall within the brief of this guide, except perhaps to mention that Córdoba's remarkable *Mezquita* is adjacent to a huge heronry! Suffice to say, you could easily spend a week in each of those cities without a chance of seeing everything.

Almería Province

This Province occupies the driest, most southeasterly corner of Iberia and resembles North Africa more closely than it does any other part of Europe. The most usual landscape is one of arid desert with sudden *barrancos* — they would be called *wadis* just across the Mediterranean — or dried-up watercourses carving defiles across the rolling plains. There is little agriculture in the interior, except where the awful plastic greenhouses which proliferate on the coastal plain, have spread inland.

The scenery then is a harsh landscape with *esparto* grass, low shrubs and aromatic herbs and very low human population.

The coast has some impressive cliffs north of the Cabo de Gata, but with coalmining and its resultant pollution a little further north at Carboneras. Beyond lies the resort of Mojacar and some nice stretches of coast. To the west of the Cabo you meet successively: a short unspoilt coastal plain, Almería City, a stretch of beach resorts (aropund Roquetas), then the interminable plastic greenhouses which stretch as far as Adra. Ornithologically, Almería is the European stronghold of Trumpeter Finch, has important populations of some steppe species, notably Dupont's Lark and Black-bellied Sandgrouse whilst the coastal lagoons host Spain's best numbers of White-headed Duck. The saltpans at the Cabo de Gata provide roosting areas for important gatherings of Audouin's Gull and are a major migration staging-post for waders, terns and the like.

The coast here juts out promisingly to the east and sea-watching can be rewarding.

The region, as with others in this guide, is under-watched and surprises could yet be in store.

Almería site A: Gata Area (Map 1)

The Cabo de Gata is at the extreme southeastern corner of Spain giving a unique situation for the reception of trans-Mediterranean migrants. Couple with this a large and moderately undisturbed area of saltpans, a wild, rocky headland and some extensive, uncultivated plains and you have a receipe for one of the truly great birding areas of Europe. The sites to consider are best dealt with separately as follows:

The Cabo

The road takes sightseers out to the lighthouse and starts off promisingly along the coast northwards, but is soon barred by a chain and you can only proceed on foot — or bike — if you wish to explore further. The gulleys along this whole stretch of coast are the winter haunt of the elusive Trumpeter Finch which flock during the colder months. Around the lighthouse you may find flocks of Rock Sparrow, and will be almost sure to come across Black Wheatear and Blue Rock Thrush. Migrants may lurk in the sparsely vegetated gulleys at suitable times, whilst Peregrine and Bonelli's Eagles breed on the cliffs, the latter being discrete and hard to see. Sea-watching may well bring shearwaters, skuas and Gannet, as well as substantial tern passage, during April, May and September in particular. The chances of a stray Lesser Crested Tern are better than average here, especially during May.

Salinas de Gata

The saltpans are worth a look at almost any time holding a substantial Audouin's Gull roost almost all year. This is to be seen at the extreme southeastern end of the pans from the hamlet of La Almadrava where you can clamber up a little bank and view from a distance of perhaps fifty metres on most days.

Further back along the salinas you will find a nicely kept hide maintained by the *Medio Ambiente*. From here a telescope is essential but the variety of waders can be great and passage times can bring almost anything.

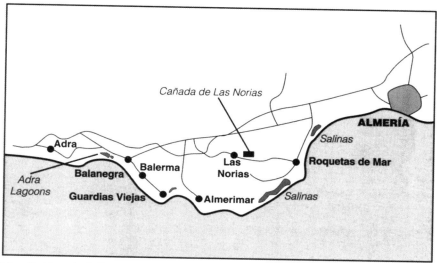

Map 2. Almería Salinas.

2. Salinas Viejas and Salinas de Cerillos

This is a big stretch of disused salinas which is accessible from an indifferent coastal path westwards from Roquetas. Needless to say, this is a good approach-direction in morning light conditions but you can also view other parts of this big area from the northwest corner where reedbeds are interesting and often seem to hold good numbers of warblers and Nightingales. The whole area is worthy of a close study.

3. Salinas de Guardias Viejas

This Salina is some eight kilometres west of the last site and needs a considerable detour to approach it as you have to go inland before striking off south just to the west of El Ejido for Guardias Viejas, from where the remains of the salinas are to the left of the road. Neglect is rapidly turning these saltpans into a reedbed, but there is a high potential for migrants here as at the other sub-sites and they should repay a careful study.

Practical Points

This is one area where a 'combination-holiday' could be rewarding and non-birding members of a party could be left to the joys of Roquetas' resort facilities providing an inexpensive 'package deal' option. There are any number of hotels for the independent traveller but they may well be busy in the peak summer months. A winter holiday may well be worthy of consideration here. As elsewhere, tracks soon become unusable after rain.

4. Almería Site D: Cañada de las Norias

This unlikely looking area here produces a site of the highest quality and potential. Assuming you are heading west along the N340 from Almería, look for a left turn signposted to 'Mojonera' from where you must turn right for Las Norias. After perhaps five kilometres you will see a long straight road striking off to the right into an industrial area. From this road you can view the first and smallest pit, on your right, without leaving the road. This often holds a White-headed Duck or two and a few warblers, etc. Go back to the main road and continue towards Las Norias. Where the road sweeps around to the left you will see the 'Cañada' (reedbed) on the right, an extensive earth-extraction pit

15

with many shallow pools, that will repay a careful morning's search, besides the resident White-headed Duck, Pochard, Grebes, etc. There are also small numbers of Marbled Duck, which may, however, be hard to find in the dense cover. Warblers and various passerine migrants can be plentiful and Lesser Short-toed Lark breed around the shore as do Little Ringed Plover. Passage waders can include almost anything and a major rarity is just waiting to be found there.

Practical points
The road from Mojonera to Las Norias, though relatively minor, is fast and therefore dangerous. Great care should accompany any manoeuvres.

Tracks around the cañada are certainly best traversed on foot and wellies may well be helpful at almost any time.

Considerable conservation efforts have been made at this sensitive site and vehicular access, though not currently prohibited, is unlikely to improve the site and should be avoided.

Accommodation is plentiful in Roquetas except during the peak season.

Almería Site E: Adra Lagoons
Taking the N340 from Almería to Adra, some 7k short of the latter, the road begins to skirt the coastal plain running alongside a rocky escarpment much quarried and with a view across acres of horrendous plastic ghreenhouses stretching over to the beach. (It's all your fault for buying their tomatoes!)

When the obvious big reed- and tree-fringed lagoon shows up on the left, prepare to take a left turn BEFORE the lagoon, down a steep slip-road. You will find well-maintained tracks between all the greenhouses, one bringing you to the edge of the lagoon. From this end you need to be viewing in the morning for the best light conditions and a telescope is essential. Take every opportunity of obtaining elevation, be it a pile of drainpipes, a heap of rotting vegetation or the roof of your car, and you should have little trouble finding White-headed Duck here where there is a population probably in excess of 70 pairs. The reeds may well hold a variety of 'skulkers' and the open water can be good for grebes and duck. An Audouin's Gull roost is regular towards the far end and they also pass along the coast with regularity hereabouts.

The greenhouses occasionally give way to small reedy areas and there is another, smaller lagooon just to the west which also has White-headed Duck. The whole area is under threat, not least from agricultural chemicals, the evidence of which you can see in the frequent discarded drums.

Practical points
The N340 is something of a racetrack, though better now that the motorway is built. If you approach westwards along the latter you will have to leave it at Punete del Rio and double back on the N340 to reach the site.

Be careful not to block any access roads, particularly as the site is regularly patrolled by police, presumably on the lookout for Melon rustlers! Large dogs also appear here and there, but thankfully are usually chained up.

Accommodation is scarce in the immediate area, but a few kilometres beyond Adra the village of El Pozuelo is the site of the friendly little Hotel Beatriz which offers a good standard of comfort and sea-watching from the balconies!

Plate 1. *Laguna de la Fuenta de Piedra Nature Reserve, Andalucía*   *Ross MacLeod*

Plate 2. *Cabo De Gata - Almería*   *G.D & Y.S Dean*

Plate 3. *Sierra De Cazorla*   *Mike Lane*

Plate 4. *Sierra Nevada*   *Mike Lane*

Granada Province

A largely inland Province, Granada contains Spain's highest mountains and has a climate dominated by this fact. Although it shares the famous Laguna de Fuente de Piedra and its Flamingoes with Málaga Province the majority of the birding to be found in Granada is in mountain areas which range from the rolling, sunlit hills of the Alpujarras to the Alpine screes and rocks of the Sierra Nevada.

The city of Granada will be on all but the most avid and single-minded birder's itinerary, with its fabulous Alhambra and many other treasures.

There is more than ample accommodation and food there but in midsummer and in the ski season it may well be hard to obtain lodgings between the city and the Sierra Nevada.

Granada Site A: Alpujarras

Really a region rather than a specific site this, it is one which merits more than a passing glance. The eastern end actually intrudes into Almería Province and the road westwards from the town of Berja is interesting. Where the road crosses a new reservoir, Rock Sparrows are regular and fields near the town are good for their rarer(!) relative, the Tree Sparrow. This is also a very good area for Rollers and the orchards hold Rufous Bush Robins in late spring.

Further west the main road (C333) northwest towards Órjiva is worth more than a cursory glance. On the ascent from Albuñol any of the little gullies bridged by the road may hold lots of migrants, especially in March and April, with a good chance of locally scarce birds like Wood Warbler. Some of the bridges are home to Red-rumped Swallows and White-rumped Swift have been found here. Higher up Woodlark and Bonelli's Warbler sing whilst Golden and Bonelli's Eagles both breed in the area. Those who wish for an all-round experience will find the spring wildflowers fascinating with several kinds of orchid making an appearance.

In conclusion, there are too many roads threaded through the valleys and across this region of high rounded hills to describe individually, but the adventurous may well find themselves rewarded in this relatively unknown part.

Practical Points

The roads in this region will require your undivided attention! In winter some may quickly become impassable. To the north there are some which lack a metalled surface indistinguishable on the maps from those which are quite decent. There is little food to be had between Albuñol and Órjiva, even if you stick to the main road.

Accommodation is plentiful in Lanjaron which is a major spa resort. From there the main road northwards to Granada is frequently slow going, thanks to lorries laden with mineral water.

Granada Site B: Sierra Nevada (Map 3)

'The Snowy Mountains' is the translation of the name of this vast region containing Spain's highest mountain, Mulhacen. There are few crags at high altitude, however, and the number and variety of raptors is disappointing when compared with much smaller ranges further west and north. They are, in fact, restricted to Golden and Bonelli's Eagles, Buzzard, Peregrines and Kestrel, with just the chance of Lesser Kestrel. Chough, however, breed commonly and one of the great specialities is the southernmost outpost in Spain of Alpine Accentor.

If you take the skiers' road to the resort of Sol y Nieve and go as high as the road permits (some 2,400 metres) you will be in the tundra-like plateau country which typifies this range and should find Alpine Accentor quite easily around the Youth Hostel and the Parador. Ibex are also found around here and other bird species which breed are Rock Sparrow, Skylark, Northern Wheatear and Black Redstart. A chance of Rock Thrush also exists. Lower down, the pinewoods hold birds typical of mountain country in the south of Spain, namely, Rock Bunting, Short-toed Treecreeper, Blue and Crested Tit, Bonelli's and Subalpine Warbler. Black-eared Wheatear are common enough and flocks of Ring Ouzel winter in the high valleys. Rocky ravines are numerous within reasonable hiking distance of the road, especially off the Purche valley, from where an obvious limestone track leads down into a spectacular gorge. Here Black Wheatear and, reputedly, Eagle Owl, are to be found.

Down in Granada itself a visit to the deservedly famous Alhambra will also yield up a few species with Blackcap, Firecrest and Crossbill (all year round), Crag Martins (winter) and Pallid Swift (summer) in the vicinity.

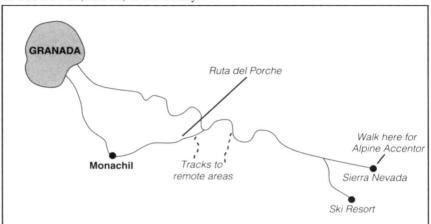

Map 3. Sierra Nevada

Practical points
The road to the ski resorts is very good and advice will be available in winter as to whether or not chains are required. It should go without saying that a walking expedition at the altitudes prevalent there is not to be undertaken lightly as weather can change rapidly and spectacularly, a sunny day suddenly becoming a pea-souper. Temperatures can plunge equally quickly and I have worn full winter gear up there in June — and still been cold!

Accommodation is no problem except in midsummer and, most importantly, between Christmas and Easter when skiers use up virtually the whole availability. The Hostal Ruta del Purche situated spectacularly at 1,500 metres off to the right of the Veleta road gives excellent value for money in food and simple accommodation and to sit around a roaring log fire rounds off the day's birding there in fine style.

Granada has a wide range of hotels and restaurants at surprisingly sensible prices.

Granada Site C: Hoya de Guadix and surrounding area (Map 4)
Quite an area this, and one in which it is impossible to give precise and useful itineraries due to its vastness and the vagaries of weather, light conditions and, not least, the wanderings of the birds themselves.

The overall impression one gains is of a vast semi-desert with some patches of cultivation and many abrupt heavily eroded ravines, often with clumps of trees and small reedbeds in the bottoms. Here Golden Oriole are numerous and Cetti's Warbler sing from almost any damp patch.

The Rio Gor which passes through the area has carved out the biggest of these and raptors frequenting its cliffs often include Short-toed Eagles and wandering Egyptian Vultures.

At Baños de Alicun to the north, cliffs are more rocky and hold Rock Sparrow, Chough and Peregrine, whilst nearby woods are good for warblers and flycatchers. Eagle Owl breed here too.

On the plains themselves good fortune and patience are required but breeding species include Black-bellied Sandgrouse, Little Bustard, Stone Curlew, Tawny Pipit and Larks, notably Calandra and Short-toed (common) and Dupont's (only in areas of esparto grass).

The Hoya de Baza is an area to the east more or less contiguous with the Hoya de Gaudix and possessing much the same mix of species. Any road marked on the map will be worth investigating especially those which cross uncultivated plains.

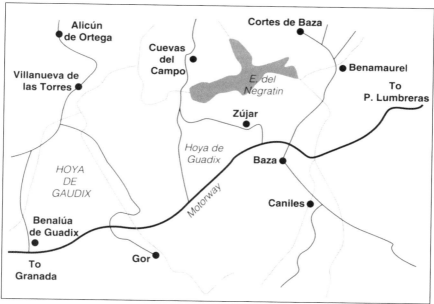

Map 4. Hoya de Gaudix and surround area.

Practical Points

As with all extensive plains, heat-haze tends to preclude midday birding in the hotter months (and 40 degrees is not unusual here in summer!).

It is worth remembering that a car is a useful hide in this sort of country — you will often see more by remaining in it.

Accommodation is plentiful in Baza and Guadix which also have some fascinating occupied cave-dwellings.

Azure-winged Magpie

Jaén Province

Olives as far as the eye can see. That sums up the rolling landscape of this province for the vast majority of its area. There are, however, a couple of mountain ranges to break the monotony and the great river Guadalquivir has its upper reaches, across the Province, dammed here and there to form long, sinuous reservoirs which themselves offer occasional birding treats.

The great range comprising the Sierras of Cazorla, Segura and Las Villas, straggles, in fact, the borders of Jaén and Granada Provinces, whilst the Sierras to the west are continuous with ranges of Córdoba Province.

The olive groves are not particularly interesting from an ornithological standpoint though they contain good numbers of common species and you may come across that Andalucían speciality, the Azure-winged Magpie, almost anywhere. The roads of the Province are often poor — there seems to be no happy medium between super-smooth highways and rough, potholed farm roads. In such a remote, un-touristy areas, the towns will not often sport much in the way of accommodation but the mountain resort of Cazorla more than makes up.

Jaén Site A: Sierra de Cazorla (Map 5)

To describe this area as a 'site' is, in fact, misleading, as the area is quite vast, comprising a massive mountain range, but it is extremely likely that most readers of this guide will find it most practical to follow, in one direction or the other, the road from Cazorla generally northwards to Franco's great dam, then turning eastwards and over the mountains to Puebla de Don Fadrique and so into Murcia Province.

Almost immediately upon leaving the 'suburbs' of the beautiful resort of Cazorla where the Hotel Andalucía, amongst others, will give you a warm welcome, you climb up through a series of hairpin bends to a 'Mirador', or viewpoint, which is possibly the best single spot in the whole area from which to observe raptors. Griffon Vultures often glide past here at eye-level and there have been fairly recent records of Lammergeier, though this small, relict population is now extinct. There are, in fact, current efforts to re-introduce this spectacular species. Other raptors, however, occur in good variety both as residents and on passage, when they may be watched coursing along the ridges at both seasons.

Next you descend into the park proper where hunting is strictly controlled — your car will already have been scrutinised at the barrier on the way up — and Red, Roe and Fallow Deer and Wild Boar are often to be seen. Less likely, of course, is a sight of the very nocturnal Lynx, though they are certainly found here as are lots of Beech Martens, Polecat and Red Squirrel.

Amongst the woods, Woodlark, Cirl Bunting, Nuthatch, Wryneck and Great Spotted Woodpecker are common whilst Dippers and Kingfisher whizz along the clear stream which forms the headwaters of the Guadalquivir giving the valley a strangely 'northern'

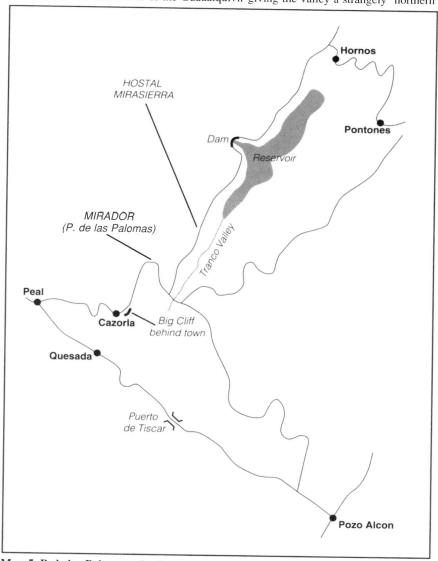

Map 5. P. de las Palomas, also Pozo Alcón

flavour. This is dispelled by the sight of big, noisy flocks of Azure-winged Magpies, here at their easternmost outpost. Citril Finch are found in winter and may breed sparingly. The dam at Tranco is worth a stop as the cliffs can hold Rock Sparrow and can be relied upon for Blue Rock Thrush and Black Wheatear whilst raptors. Chough and Raven are seen overhead. Lesser Kestrel breed sporadically. The climb up to the eastern ridge involves some concentration for the driver, then, once gained, the ridge offers more fine views as well as Rock Thrush, Northern Wheatear, Tawny Pipit and more raptors. All the roads of the area should be regarded as typical mountain roads and journeys timed accordingly.

On the way over to Puebla de Don Fadrique the village of Santiago de la Espada has a few bars where food can be obtained and there are some good cliffs in the neighbourhood which is a fine area for Egyptian Vultures, especially near the rubbish tips. Nocturnal (or lucky) visitors can find Eagle Owls almost anywhere, again worth looking for around tips.

No account of these Sierras is complete without a mention of the wildflowers for which they are renowned. April and May are the best months.

Gastronomically, trout is the local speciality and there are plenty of hotels, hostels and campsites, largely along the valley road between Cazorla and Tranco. By the side of this road, the excellent Hostal Mirasierra offers inexpensive comfort, and Wild Boar will frequently appear to feed in the car park after dinner!

Exploration on foot is, of course, very possible and mountain biking is popular on the many tracks. Land-Rover 'safaris' can be arranged in Cazorla at the Tourist Information Office but would be unlikely to appeal to most readers of this guide!

Anyone staying in the town of Cazorla will find it worthwhile to drive out on one of the roads from the back of the town to obtain a view of the huge and obvious cliff which towers over the town. This cliff has breeding Griffon Vultures, Bonelli's Eagle and Peregrine and seems to act as something of a magnet for migrating raptors, especially in early April. Each passing bird of prey tends to bring out from the cliff an anxious Peregrine or Bonelli's Eagle.

Jaén Site B: Embalses del Guadalquivir (Map 6)

The Guadalquivir has been dammed in several places forming long, sinuous reservoirs, little more than a widened river. There are three in total. By far the most easily visited and usually the most productive, is the Embalse de Puente de la Cerrada, which can be viewed by simply standing on the bridge where the dam is crossed by the road from Torreperogil to Peal de Becerro. A track runs from here eastwards along the southern side for even better views. Given appropriate water levels with just a little mud visible below the reeds you will be unlucky not to see Purple Gallinule. The reeds can hold many warblers including Great Reed and Savi's and good stretches of mud can attract hosts of waders to this out-of-the-way site. On a recent visit a Marsh Sandpiper was amongst a fine variety there. Gadwell is common and almost anything can turn up here. Pond Terrapins are numerous.

The other reservoirs are also most interesting but generally more difficult to approach, though the bridge crossing the dam at the western end of Pedro Marin can also be a good vantage point often giving good flocks of waders and gulls in early spring. Elsewhere, the height of the reeds and the lack of suitable roads make life difficult — exploration on foot is probably the order of the day.

Practical points

It is probable that many visitors will combine a visit with a stay in nearby Cazorla (Jaén: A), which has excellent facilities, but it is a mistake to rush away from a site like this without allotting at least, say, four hours, even if you are only planning to visit Puente de la Cerrada. The countryside around the reservoirs consists largely of unexciting olive groves, but most of the roads are quite fast and you can get from place to place quite

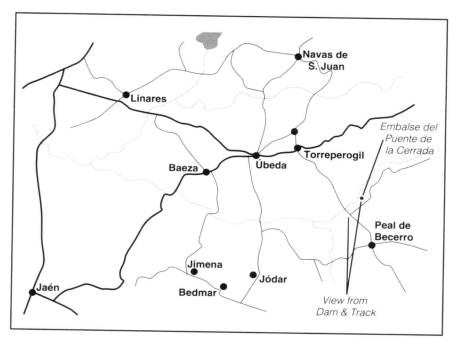

Map 6. Reservoirs of the upper Guadalquivir.

Note that some maps show a minor road running from Estación Garciez-Jimena along the south side of Pedro Marin to near Silo. This is in fact barely passable in places and is not really worthwhile as the reservoir is not approached very closely, except at one point. A telescope is essential at these sites.

Jaén Site C: Sierra de Andújar (Map 7)

If there is a paradise, it will resemble the Sierra de Andújar on a sunny April morning. Although not well endowed with rocky peaks this range of lonely rolling mountains is densely covered with evergreen oaks, other trees and Mediterranean scrub and is home to a wealth of tree-nesting raptors and a huge range of passerines. It also provides ideal conditions for lots of mammals and Red and Fallow Deer, Mouflon and Wild Baor are very common. Neither is it unusual to see a Tortoise trotting across the road in front of you — another reason to take it steadily!

Starting from the pleasant town of Andújar you have a choice as to whether to follow the long, slow route northwards over into Ciudad Real Province and to which you will need to allot a day, given any luck at all with the birds. Or you can simply take the right fork at Las Viñas and wind around the mediocre road to the dam at La Lancha. There and back is a morning's work.

Whichever you do will bring excellent chances of Black and Griffon Vulture (with the former just about predominating here), Booted, Short-toed and possibly Golden and Imperial Eagles, Goshawk and Sparrowhawk. Passerines include the abundant Azure-winged Magpie, Golden Oriole, Hawfinch, Melodious, Subalpine and Dartford Warblers and Red-rumped Swallows which breed under several bridges. There are Chough and Crag Martin at the dam

25

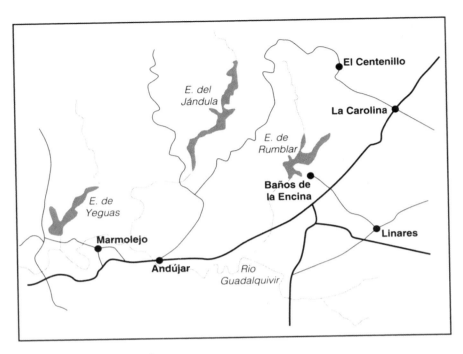

Map 7. Sierra de Andújar

Practical points

The roads in this sierra require great care being poorly surfaced (especially in the eastern parts) and very narrow.

If an area is fenced, DO NOT ENTER, as much of the region is patrolled by fighting bulls. Whatever your views on the bull's chances in the ring, a telescope and Barbour jacket are not the ideal weapons for tackling half a ton of angry and agile beast!

Hotels are to be found in Andujar, but it is worth noting that beyond Las Viñas, where there are a couple of bar-restaurants, there are no refreshment facilities for a very long way.

Jaén Site D: Sierra de la Pandera

This is a pleasant little range, easy of access and little different from the adjacent Sierra de Magina in terms of species diversity. Although the road demands care it is easily traversed from Castillo de Locubín in the south to the Provincial capital in the north, a route which passes few settlements and constantly has good country in view. On the cliffs to the north quite close to Jaén, Golden and Bonelli's Eagle and Peregrine breed and are often seen. Along the road Melodious, Sardinian, Subalpine and Dartford Warblers are all numerous and Rock Bunting, Black and Black-eared Wheatears, Roller, Bee Eater and Thekla Lark are all common.

Practical points

Allow plenty of time for the drive as the road, though usually quiet, is narrow and requires care. There is ample accommodation in Jaén.

26

Córdoba Province

A big Province, Córdoba has a vast diversity of habitat, from the wide plains of the north through the rocky sierras to the rolling farmlands of the south, interspersed with little wetlands and of major importance to the ornithologist. The Province is sliced into two halves by the River Guadalquivir, which provides in itself both a migration route and some riverine habitat.

Human population tends to be concentrated on the towns and the capital city leaving the northern plains very sparsely populated. The climate is hot, largely dry, but with more rainfall towards the west and in the sierras. Agriculture is fairly intensive throughout with much cereal production. The city of Córdoba is a world-renowned tourist attraction with all the facilities that implies.

The northern borders of the Province abut Extremadura in the west and Castilla-La Mancha in the east — a small area of the latter is treated in this guide as being readily accessible from Córdoba Province and of considerable interest.

Córdoba Site A: Córdoba (capital)

The Provincial capital has a great deal to offer the sightseeing tourist and not a little to offer the determined birder.

Park near to the Puente Romano (Roman bridge) and, on the downstream side, you will look straight into what is nothing more than an 'apartment block' for herons. Here nests a huge colony of Cattle Egrets interspersed with a good scattering of Night Herons and the odd pair of Squacco Herons. They are largely in big eucalyptus trees on islands in the centre of the usually sluggish Guadalquivir.

The reeds which line the river are home to Little Bittern, Penduline and Bearded Tit, Great Reed and Cetti's Warblers and, with luck, Purple Gallinule, whilst almost anything can occur on passage.

Lesser Kestrel nest sparingly amongst the many Jackdaw on the ancient buildings. This site presents a unique opportunity to appease non-birding party members who will be enchanted by the amazing Mezquita.

Practical points

Traffic in Córdoba is horrendous! Park in one of the pay car parks at either end of the Roman bridge and your few pesetas will be well spent.

Córdoba has a great many hotels, but be warned that Easter week is almost invariably booked up well in advance.

Córdoba Site B: Sierra de Hornachuelos

A site consisting largely of lowish mountains covered in open oak woods and Mediterranean scrub, though with a few interesting rocky gorges. All the usual raptors are to be found and woodland birds include Hawfinch and Golden Oriole. Black Stork breed in small numbers and the immediate neighbourhood of Hornachuelos village is as good a place as any to get a sight of one.

Wolves, Lynx and Mongoose still occur here.

It may be best to attempt a round-trip by taking the C0142 north from Hornachuelos and returning by way of Las Navas de la Concepción.

Practical points

Catering establishments in this lonely area are few and far between as are gas stations. There is ample accommodation in Córdoba some 55 km to the east and in Écija to the south.

It may be worth bearing in mind that the latter town has — and deserves — the reputation of being the hottest town in Europe!

Córdoba Site C: Lagunas de Zóñar, Rincon and Amarga

1. Zóñar (Map 8)

One of the few lagoons that has permanent water, Zóñar's levels nevertheless fluctuate with rainfall. When it is very full with no visible mud under the reeds, you will require patience, especially in the breeding season, to see the speciality, Purple Gallinule. Given lower water levels, they are easy. The reeds hold Great Reed Warbler and other species and the open water plays host to visiting wildfowl including White-headed Duck, which used to breed. For some reason the lagoon seems to exercise an attraction over raptors and a wide variety can be seen passing over. On one visit I had five species in half an hour.

The Information Centre seems always to be closed but the wardens of the Medio Ambiente do ask people to stay away from the reedbeds and a sign in two languages requests this.

For the best views take a track to the right which crosses over the railway near the eastern end of the lagoon. This track is very muddy after rain!

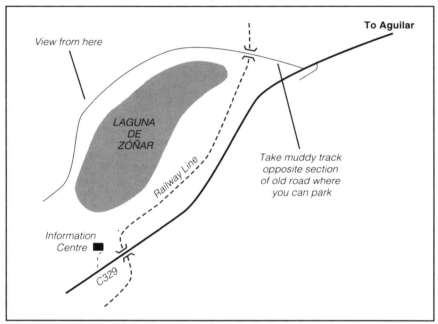

View from here

To Aguilar

LAGUNA DE ZÓÑAR

Railway Line

Take muddy track opposite section of old road where you can park

Information Centre

C329

Map 8. Lagoon Zóñar

2. Rincon (Map 9)

This is a semi-permanent lagoon, set amongst vineyards and approached on an unmade track which again quickly becomes impassable after rain. If there are wardens at the Information Centre, they will be most helpful and will let you have the key to the public hide. If not, just walk around the perimeter fence. In the right water conditions, White-headed Duck and Purple Gallinule may be present. Passerines frequent the lush vegetation and Marsh Harriers are regular winter visitors.

3. Amarga (Map 10)

This site actually comprises two lagoons: the Laguna Dulce (sweet) and Amarga (bitter). the former is immediately visible as you park your car in the roadside car park. A bare, roundish depression, it is apt to dry up quite rapidly, but the Amarga, a kilometre's walk up a pleasant little path, holds more-or-less permanent water and a good growth of aquatic vegetation. The birds you are likely to see here are much the same as those mentioned for the other two lagoons.

Practical points

There is ample accommodation along the road south from Córdoba and the Hotel Castillo de Montemayor is highly recommended. A short walk from that hotel on an April evening will take you to the eponymous castle which has a few pairs of Scops Owls!

Córdoba Site D: The Plains of Northern Córdoba

The vast area where the Province borders on Badajóz, Extremadura, has the character of that region and many of its birds.

The road from Blazquez to Campillo de Llerena, also IJinojsa travels through the typical 'dehesa' country so beloved of Azure-winged Magpies, Black-shouldered Kites and wintering Cranes. Extensive cereal fields here and in the neighbourhood of Honojosa del Duque give an excellent chance of winter flocks and breeding pairs of both Bustards, both Great and Little, are relatively common. Montagu's Harriers and Black Kites are especially numerous in spring and summer.

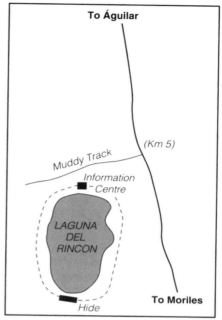

Map 9. Lagoon Rincon.

Black-shouldered Kite

29

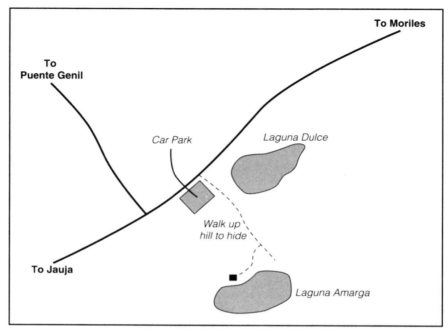

Map 10. Lagoons Dulce and Amarga.

Other raptors often seen over the area include Red Kite, Griffon and Black Vultures and all the eagle species. The roads from Zújar to Belalcazar and on eastwards to Santa Eufemia are quiet and have been very productive in the past. Spanish Sparrow are numerous here and any sparrows nesting in the base of the many White Stork nests are worth checking out, though House Sparrows do this too. Spanish Sparrows often flock around field margins as well. Calandra Larks are conspicuously common. In very early spring Great Spotted Cuckoo seem to be frequent and it is possible that they winter in the region. They are certainly harder to find as the year progresses.

Practical points

The usual comments about heat-haze apply especially here if midday expeditions are attempted.

Hotels are to be found in all major towns with several in Pozoblanco.

Sevilla Province

Sevilla is really a Province of two parts. East of the great river Guadalquivir, it is a largely agricultural region — one of rolling farmlands with just a few interesting lagoons, relics of a once wild and exciting land. To the west is the famous wilderness of the Coto Doñana, which, however, we shall treat cursorily in this guide. Everything that can be written about this great river delta has already been written, so it and its surroundings will be the subject of a short section, like other less important sites.

The Sevilla to Córdoba motorway is fast and good and most of the other roads of the Province are sound.

Sevilla is a beautiful, cosmopolitan city, with a cathedral ranking amongst the finest in the world and many Moorish treasures. It is the home of Flamenco and the original thing can still be found in the little bars of Triana, the Gypsy suburb, across the river from the city. The Easter parade in Sevilla is world-famous and it is quite useless to try and find a room there during or around that and other local fiestas. Smaller towns may well be worth a try even during those periods and even within a few short kilometres of the capital. I have, indeed, found plentiful accommodation in towns such as Estepa and Écija when Sevilla was chock-full.

Sevilla Site A: Carmona area

This is a rolling area of cereal fields which supports relics of once-numerous 'steppe' species, especially in the winter months.

Little Bustard is present all year round, though often elusive, hiding well in growing crops. In winter there is always a chance of a wandering Great Bustard.

Montagu's Harrier patrol the fields in spring and summer and the vegetation along the many little streams forms 'oases' which can hold warblers, etc. at migration times.

Practical points

Hotels in Carmona include a splendid 'Parador de Turismo', but this is probably an area you will want to visit whilst en route between, say, the Coto Doñana and more easterly sites.

Little Bustard

Heat-haze is a potential problem, as elsewhere, and the best times for birding are early and late in the day.

Sevilla Site B: Sierra Morena

At the most northerly point of the Province, the Sierra Morena sweeps along the border the Badajóz Province. This is an area of wooded hills with a population of tree-nesting raptors. Booted Eagles can be numerous and there is a chance of Golden and Imperial as well as Goshawk and Sparrowhawk. Black Vulture is relatively frequent overhead.

The 'dehesa' country here is especially rich in passerines with breeding Azure-winged Magpies very common. Bonelli's Warblers, Cirl Buntings and Woodlark are characteristic and winter flocks of Redwing and Song Thrush are the norm.

Practical points

The whole region is criss-crossed by lots of minor roads and a 'random' approach may well prove effective. The area around Guadalcanal has proved productive in the past.

Accommodation in the area itself is limited, but readers will probably visit this region en route between sites further south and the plains of Extremadura.

Fenced areas should not be entered as bull ranches cover parts of these hills and if the bull doesn't get you, the farmer probably will!

Sevilla Site C (part in Huelva Province): Coto Doñana (maps 11&12)

The 'Coto' has been described as Western Europe's last great wilderness and so it remains despite, in recent years, severe water shortages caused by water extraction further up the Guadalquivir for irrigation. Natural drought has also played a part in converting original marshland into desert.

Undoubtedly a site of crucial importance to the wildlife which lives there, but the Coto Doñana can be a disappointing experience for the visiting birder who may well find the best sites around its periphery.

An immense amount has been written about this region in the last thirty years and it is not the business of this guide to provide any detailed information, but the most accessible sites may be summarised as follows:

1. The Bridge at El Rocio – This is a site where you can, with patience, see almost all of the specialities of the Coto and is a fairly reliable spot for Spoonbill, Marbled Duck and herons, as well as terns and waders. The site is actually just to the south of El Rocio on the road towards Matalascanas.

2. Centro de Information de la Rocina – Here, a little way south of the last site, you take an entrance on the right and find a well-manned Visitor Centre with up-to-date information available in several languages and a nature trail of interest throughout the year. In autumn and winter Ferruginous and White-headed Ducks may be found here and Glossy Ibis is also a possibility. During the breeding season passerines can be very good here, with a nice variety of warblers in particular.

3. El Acebuche — Here, well to the south along the same road, is a much bigger Information Centre with a shop and Cafeteria and probably the tamest Azure-winged Magpies you will encounter! Another nature trail leads to some good hides overlooking reedy ponds with good chances of Purple Gallinule, as well as herons, etc. Your chances of Black-shouldered Kite in this area are also good.

4. Back through the town of El Rocio, a poor sandy track leads out to the Boca del Lobo (Wolf's mouth), from where a good overall view over the Marismas can be obtained. This is possibly the best site for a view of Imperial Eagle.

Otherwise the visitor can book Land Rover excursions into restricted areas, either by enquiring at one of the Information Centres, or by calling (955 – provincial code) 430432.

Within the reserve there are a variety of habitat types, many of which are replicated in

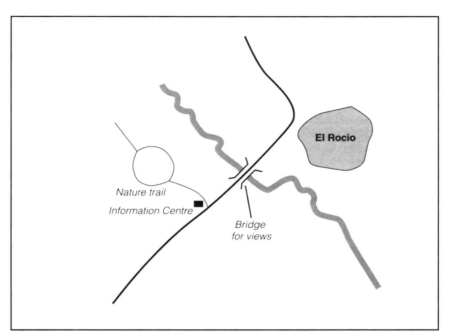

Map 11. El Rocio.

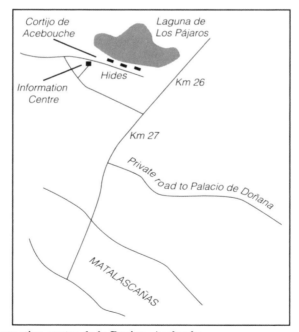

Map 12. Information centre de la Rocina, Acebuche.

33

the surrounding areas, but it is the sheer size and remoteness of the area which renders it so important and these factors tend to militate against a successful birding visit.

All seasons are important, the winter particularly so, when vast flocks of Greylag Geese and Cranes put in an appearance.

The breeding population of Spanish Imperial Eagle is probably around 4 pairs and other rare and endangered species include such diverse ones as Marbled Duck, Pin-tailed Sandgrouse and, if you believe in fairies, Andalucían Hemipode. Raptors, notably Black Kite, are everywhere and breeding mammals include Lynx and Mongoose.

Practical points

The resort of Matalascanas, whilst having a range of hotels, is a depressing and Godforsaken dump, whose very existence is thought by many to be a disgrace. Accommodation exists at El Rocio and Almonte, but it is very important to check that your spring visit does NOT coincide with the great Gypsy Fiesta, when no sum of money will buy you a room.

The National Park authorities strictly discourage any form of trespass within the boundaries of the Park — stick to public roads.

Imperial Eagle

Huelva Province

Although this Province, the most southerwesterly of Spain, falls outside the main scope of this guide, some mention should be made of it, for sake of completeness.

That part of the Coto Doñana which falls within Huelva's boundaries is described under the heading of Sevilla, Site C.

That apart, the main ornithological interest in Huelva lies along its coast, where several small estuaries are to be found creating some nice little wetlands. The Marismas of Odiel, just across the river from the Provincial capital, sports an important Spoonbill colony and any of these sites can be of great interest at passage times and in winter when any prominent spot can be productive as a sea-watching venue. Shearwaters and petrels can be regular at these places.

Inland, the Sierra Morena continues (see Sevilla Site B), with much the same mix of species, to and beyond the Portuguese frontier. In this wild area you stand good chances of Black Stork, Black Vulture and other montane species, Red-rumped Swallows are very common and White-rumped Swift have been reported.

There is plenty of accommodation in Huelva and some very good campsites along the coast including one overlooking the sand-spit at El Rompido, reached from the town of Cartaya.

Black Stork

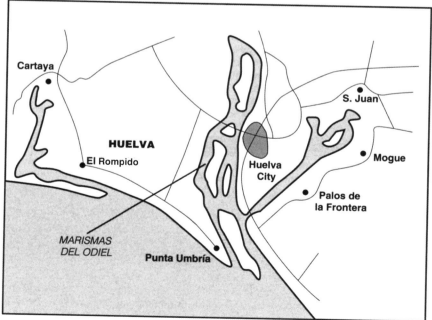

Map 13. The Marismas del Odiel and Huelva, El Rompido.

35

Griffon Vulture

Cádiz Province

In simple terns, Cádiz has something for everyone. The mountains inland are alive with raptors, the lagoons scattered around the coastal plains are home to some of Europe's rarest birds, the coast is visited by windblown seabirds and the migration of raptors and other species is amongst the most spectacular in the world.

Tarifa is the southernmost place in Europe and the point where the Atlantic meets the Mediterranean. The African coast of Morocco can be seen very clearly on most days and it is around here that the raptor passage can be seen to its best advantage in spring and autumn. Nearby La Janda is only a relic of its former expansive plain but still holds some good birds and in the nearby sierras the rear White-rumped Swift may be found. Further inland the sierras are excellent for raptors, whilst up the bank of the Guadalquivir are the pinewoods of Bonanza where many of the best birds of the Coto Doñana, just across the river, come visiting. One of the few problems with Cádiz is drought. In dry years many of the lagoons are apt to dry out completely, which can totally alter the character of the site.

Access to Gibraltar's British colony may be achieved at the horrendous town of La Linea (where, however, Common Bulbul have bred in the park), but unless you are going to watch for migrating raptors from the Rock's elevation, or 'tick' the Barbary Partridges, Gibraltar has little to commend it. Algeciras is also something of a dump but has plenty of cheap accommodation and restaurants. This cannot be said for Sanlucar de Barrameda which is not a town for cheap eateries (Jerez is much better). It is also worth pointing out at this stage that, at the time of writing, the motorway from Cádiz to Sevilla is a toll-road, one of the few in the South of Spain.

There are plenty of potential diversions in Cádiz including the sherries and riding-school of Jerez and the possibility of a day trip to Tangier from Algeciras. The Atlantic beaches west of Tarifa are also very clean and extensive.

It may be stressed here that the inclusion of a site under this Provincial heading — or others, for that matter — in no way suggests that it is necessarily superior to some of the sites which, for reasons of space have been exluded. There are lagoons dotted all over the place and little rocky sierras too, many of which would repay exploration. We can only describe what we hope is a representative selection.

Cádiz Site A: Tarifa area

It is only ten miles over to Africa from this, the most southerly point of Europe and the point where the Mediterranean and the Atlantic meet. In clear weather you can see much detail of the Moroccan countryside across the narrow strait.

Seawatching can be very good here in March/April and September/October particularly, but also in winter, though Tarifa town hardly lends itself to this activity as you cannot find sufficient elevation for a grandstand view and better opportunities exist further west and from Gibraltar. Behind the town, along the coast road, huge windfarms dominate the landscape making for a surreal aspect. In truth, the immediate area was never particularly pretty anyway, being little more than bare, rolling downland, but the major attraction, ornithologically speaking, is the annual migration of raptors (and storks) across the Straits; the weather conditions dictate the precise landfall of the bulk of the spring migrants. They tend to arrive from the south over the Moroccan coast and ride up on thermals to great heights before gliding over the water. Therefore, in strong westerlies, they will drift in over the Rock and can be seen well from either the elevation of Gibraltar itself or as they filter inland, often up the valley towards Ronda. In easterly conditions they may well strike land anywhere between Tarifa and the mouth of the Guadalquivir, which many will then follow inland. The trick is to anticipate the landfall and be there for the mid-afternoon peak.

There is a substantial resident population of Griffon Vultures in the low sierras behind the coast, but the real interest here must be the migration, by no means restricted to raptors. Almost everything can turn up and to present a list of potential species would be futile.

Practical points

The coast road is almost always busy and invariably has a big Guardia Civil presence with radar traps almost anywhere.

Tarifa has a big range of hotels and others are to be found along the highway. Algeciras and La Linea also have accommodation, but both, and particularly the latter, have all the beauty of Runcorn or possibly Calais.

Should you be tempted to cross to Gibraltar you will find the crossing point at La Linea very congested at times when the Spanish workers are going over, and possibly at other times if the Border Police are making one of their frequent 'points'. Still, you will need to go in if you wish to tick Barbary Partridge . . .

Cádiz Site B: Zahara/Tahivilla (Map 14)

Westwards along the coast road from Tarifa you soon come to a low-lying but slightly undulating area in the depression of which lies La Janda, once a major wetland and wilderness site, housing the last Cranes to breed in southwest Europe, as well as many

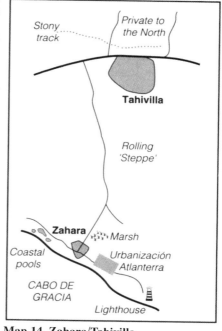

Map 14. Zahara/Tahivilla.

other sensitive species. Now reclaimed for agriculture, it still exercises some attraction for birds, especially for wintering bustards — both species being present in small numbers in most winters. Raptors are a feature of the area, both at passage times and in winter, whilst the many ditches can be good for waders, wildfowl and passerines, particularly wagtails and pipits, which always seem to be present in vast numbers at appropriate times.

Raptors probably drift over from their breeding sites in the local sierras also and a considerable variety can be seen there, even including Imperial Eagle on a recent visit, whilst Black-shouldered Kite puts in an occasional appearance in winter.

Zahara de los Atunes is a little beach resort and there is rolling steppe country between here and Tahivilla, in which Little Bustard again may be found.

Zahara itself has a nice, if sometimes malodorous, little estuary — virtually any species of wader can turn up there and there have been records of the rarer crakes there, as at the bigger Barbate estuary, a little to the west.

You can then travel east back along the coast to Atlantera where White-rumped Swift have apparently bred in a conspicuous abandoned hotel. Making your way on through sprawling urbanisations you come to a lighthouse and an area rich in migration potential and excellent for both sea-watching and in the right wind, raptor passage.

Practical points

The tracks across La Janda are very rough and stony. The north of the area is generally private and has to be viewed from the unrestricted roads through a telescope. There is considerable agricultural activity throughout.

Zahara has plenty of hotels and hostels — the Hostal Almadraba is well-positioned, comfortable and reasonably priced.

Cádiz Site C: Laguna de Medina

Just outside the Sherry capital of Jerez, this is a site of major importance which, however, varies with the amount of water from year to year. All you have to do here is park in the designated car park and walk around the outside of a well-maintained perimeter fence. The huge lagoon usually has a small population of White-headed Ducks and both Crested Coot and Purple Gallinule have bred in recent years. Outside the breeding season numbers of Flamingo have been as high as 800 and Marbled Duck may also flock there. Black-necked and Great-crested Grebes are dotted over the water and you should also see Red-crested Pochard and other wildfowl. In winter their numbers can be spectacular.

Practical points

A telescope is essential here as distances are great. If you plan to walk right around the lagoon you will need to allow at least a whole morning — and bear in mind that it can get very hot here! After rain, wellies will be needed.

There are all tourist facilities in Jerez.

Cádiz Site D: Lagunas de Terry, Puerto de Santa Maria (Maps 15 & 16)

Given a half-reasonable prior rainfall, this is one of Andalucia's best little sites, with a good chance of Crested Coot, and many other species. There are, in fact, three lagoons (see map). Approaching the largest of them, the Laguna Salada, is a matter of picking your way along the edge of a field or two, assuming the Medio Ambiente's entrance is closed, and viewing over a barbed-wire fence. As you get close, you may well hear Lesser Short-toed and Calandra Larks in the surround fields. The lagoon itself is an excellent site for Crested Coot, and often holds White-headed Duck, as well as terns and Pratincoles. Purple Gallinule and Little Bittern have bred, and, outside the breeding season, Marbled Duck

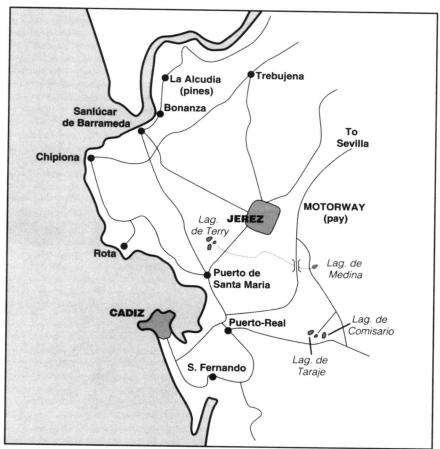

Map 15. Jerez and surrounding area.

Cádiz Site E: Laguna de Taraje (Map 15)

A relatively unfrequented lagoon set amongst quiet pinewoods and open field, this site is usually worth a visit and there are actually two more lagoons in the immediate area. Taraje, however, is the biggest and most accessible of them. Travelling eastwards from Puerto Real on the road to Paterna de Rivera you strike off on a good but unsurfaced track through the pines near to the 9 km stone. Take the right fork after just over a kilometre and the lake comes up on your right set in a hollow depression. There is much vegetation around the edges and Purple Gallinule are only one of the species that can be found here. Wildfowl are often well represented and may include the odd 'goodie' like White-headed Duck or Marbled Duck. Crested Coot put in the occasional appearance here, raptors pass with some frequency and Golden Oriole are amongst the birds you may see in the woods nearby.

A track around the perimeter to the east leads you to another track to the south which in turn leads to the Laguna de San Antonio.

The other lagoon, the Laguna de Comisario, is usually less interesting and is reached by a footpath from the same road a little further east.

39

Practical points

The footpaths can be quite muddy in rainy seasons. When parking you must take care not to block farm tracks which are extensively used here. Jerez is probably best for accommodation locally.

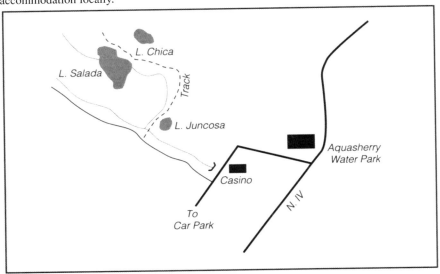

Map 16. Lagunas de Terry.

Cádiz Site F: Lagunas de Espera (Map 17)

This is a whole complex of little lagoons between Espera and las Cabezas de San Juan reached on roads which are not shown on all maps. They are well worth the trouble and can hold some of the local specialities at any season. These include Purple Gallinule and Crested Coot, for which the lagoons may well be the best site. Flamingo are usually present and the autumn is best for Marbled Duck. Passage waders almost certainly feature Black-tailed Godwit and Orphean Warbler are often found in pines in the area.

To approach the main three lagoons drive north through Espera on the C343 and look for a left turn towards Las Cabezas de San Juan. After some 1.8 km, another left turn on a surfaced road takes you to the Laguna Hondilla. Further on lies the larger Laguna Salada de Zorrilla and yet further, almost due south of the last, the Laguna Dulce de

Map 17. Lagunas de Espera, L . del Taraje.

Plate 5. *Coastal scrub Adjacent to Roquetas de Mar*

G.D & Y.S Dean

Plate 6. *El Rocio Bridge*

Mike Lane

Plate 7. *Steppe Country - Almeria, ideal habitat for Black-bellied Sandgrouse.*   Roger Powellr

Plate 8. *Lagunas De Alcazar, San Juan*   Mike Lane

Zorrilla. Three smaller pools are to be found to the northwest towards Las Cabezas but the three mentioned above are always more likely to yield some good birds.

Practical points

The landowners here are apt to restrict access without warning and it is always best to ask the locals before entering fields, etc. A polite approach will usually secure entry unless there are good reasons for preventing it. The lagoons are apt to dry up later in the year when they will be quite useless, though in some years water will remain throughout.

Jerez is the best town for accommodation locally, though there is a Parador de Turismo at Arcos de la Frontera.

Cádiz Site G: La Algaida and Bonanza

Leaving Bonanza to the north of Sanlucar de Barrameda simply stay as close to the Guadalquivir as you can and you will inevitably arrive at the Salinas de Sanlucar. These are private properties and it is necessary to ask permission to enter. In the winter months when salt-extraction activities are limited and usually during spring, a permit will be issued but you MUST call at the offices immediately you enter the gate. The salinas are situated right by the river, which is a major migration route, and almost anything can show up there. Waders can be impressive and gulls and terns always worth scanning for rarities.

Back to the main road you can head north towards the pinewoods, a beautiful stand of 'umbrella' pines, known as La Algaida. Every migrant species of western Europe seems to congregate here and fidning them amongst the dense canopy can be a most challenging and very rewarding experience, as raptors stream overhead almost all the time, with Black Kite at almost pest proportions. Azure-winged Magpie and Short-toed Treecreeper are common and Raven are also ever present.

When you emerge from the woods out into a harsh empty plain, you soon regain the riverbank and need to plan for a few hours of very slow motoring, checking the many little ponds and marshes and scanning the huge plains. Any of the residents of the Coto Doñana can and do drift over the river and raptors hunt over these plains in some profusion. Both species of sandgrouse occur and Collared Pratincole are numerous, as, usually, are Gull-billed Tern.

The road eventually emerges at Los Palacios de Villafranca.

Practical points

The road is BAD. Potholes like opencast coalmines are the norm and will slow you down if the birds don't!

Flies are a nuisance within the pinewoods so keep your car windows shut if you stop.

There are no facilities of any kind between Bonanza and Los Palacios. Make sure you have supplies and fuel for the journey.

Sanlucar is a touch restricted as far as accommodation and cheap food is concerned but Jerez is much better.

Cádiz Site H: Bay of Cádiz

The whole shore of the Bay of Cádiz is one mass of saltmarsh with a wide intertidal zone and lots of roosting and feeding potential for waders. It can be viewed from many points along the main road into the busy port from the southeast and also on the big sweep of the bay northwards towards El Puerto de Santa Maria.

It is the main breeding area in the whole of Spain for Little Tern and numbers of waders can be very large.

Wintering wildfowl include flocks of Pintail and Wigeon and seabirds tend to shelter in the bay in westerly gales. The Cádiz seawall is the standard spot for sea-watching.

White-headed Duck

Practical points

The main coast roads are enormously busy and care must be taken if seeking places to stop or turn off.

Ample accommodation may be found in Cádiz.

Cádiz Site J: Sierras de Ubrique and Grazalema

These sunny and outstandingly attractive low mountains house some of Europe's best concentrations of raptors, the rocky cliffs being excellent for Bonelli's Eagle and Eagle Owls and the extensive woodland giving nesting potential for many pairs of Booted Eagle. Chough, Blue Rock Thrush and Black Wheatear are common here and Hawfinch and Golden Oriole are numerous in the woodland. Deer are everywhere and the drive through here on any spring morning is memorable.

In summer Red-necked Nightjar are to be listened for at dusk and Egyptian Vulture and Short-toed Eagle will join the resident raptors above. Rock Thrush and Bonelli's Warblers occur (the latter commonly) and there is a chance of White-rumped Swift, especially around the areas where Red-rumped Swallow are to be seen.

Practical points

Ronda is the best site of accommodation (see Malaga site C), as the villages within the area are distinctly limited in scope.

Málaga Province

The Costa del Sol's heart (if it possesses such an organ) is here with the massive and busy resorts of Torremolinos, Marbella and so forth sharing the coast with the rather unexciting modern provincial capital, which does, however, have a useful airport. Although there is the odd estuary along the coast to provide a little interest, the real gem of the Province is the little area of lowish mountain country around Rhonda. The town bearing that name is also a good place to stay having a great deal of accommodation and food and some wonderful scenery as well as excellent birding.

The sites mentioned under this provincial heading, as elsewhere, are by no means the only places where one can see good birds in Málaga and the adventurous may well find exploration of almost any likely-looking site very rewarding.

The coast road is worth avoiding at all costs, especially in summer, being extremely busy and remarkably dangerous.

The salt lake of the Fuente de Piedra is on the border of Granada Province but it is treated under Málaga in this guide.

Málaga Site A: Laguna de Fuente de Piedra (Map 18)

This is a huge, natural salt lake, once used for salt production and now the only regular breeding site for Greater Flamingo of which there can be as many as 10,000 pairs. Other breeding species in recent years have included Gull-billed Tern and Slender-billed Gull, whilst the winter months see an invasion of good flocks of wildfowl and a small, isolated wintering group of Cranes. Stone Curlew are common in the neighbourhood and waders and raptors occur on passage.

Flamingo are extremely sensitive when breeding and the site, rightly, is protected by an encircling fence. It goes without saying that you should stay outside this barrier.

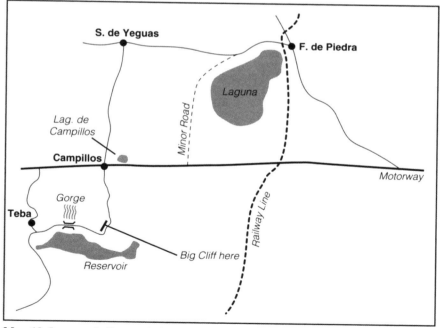

Map 18. Laguna de Fuente de Piedra.

45

There is a Visitor Centre well signposted from the village of Fuente de Piedra.

The best views of the vast lagoon are from a point just north of the westernmost extremity in the late afternoon and also at the northern end. Into the lake at both these points run fresh streams bringing a little green vegetation to the barren landscape and attracting concentrations of passerines in particular.

Practical points

The need for freedom from disturbance is paramount here and good behaviour at this site is essential. Any temporary restrictions and the instructions of the wardens must be followed carefully.

Heat-haze is a huge problem here, even at relatively early dates in the year, and a telescope is essential.

Antequera has plenty of accommodation plus Lesser Kestrels(!) and is close at hand.

Málage Site B: Laguna Dulce de Campillos (Map 18)

This site is one of many Andalucian lagoons which is of a temporary nature and when dry is of no interest whatever. After a wet winter, however, it can be highly spectacular, with relatively approachable Flamingoes, Slender-billed and other gulls, Avocets, Stilts and a good variety of migrant waders.

It may easily be seen from the N342 from which you turn on to a lay-by created from a stretch of old road. You scarcely need to get out of the car to see the birds.

There are other lagoons accessible from roads to the southwest of Campillos and shown on the maps, of which the Laguna Salada is perhaps the best, but none come quite up to the standard of the Laguna Dulce (Sweet lake) and are apt to dry up more readily.

Practical points

Helpful points about this site are its aspect, which permits viewing from the lay-by at most times of day and its small size which enables you to see most of the birds well.

There are two small hotels, at least, in Campillos and many in nearby Antequera.

Málage Site C: Teba (Map 18)

Approaching Teba on the C342 from Campillos, you first come across a big obvious cliff on the right-hand side which has breeding Griffon Vultures, Chough, Raven and Alpine Swift. After a good stop to admire this site make your way towards Ronda until you come to an iron-railed bridge over the Rio la Venta. This is at the foot of the famous Teba Gorge, through which the stream flows. On the nearby cliffs at the flanks of the Gorge, Bonelli's Eagle breed, and at passage times is often seen sallying forth to 'intercept' migrant raptors which pass through frequently.

Chough, Blue Rock Thrush, Black Wheatear, Rock Dove and Rock Sparrow are all numerous, there are Grey Wagtails along the stream and the streamside vegetation holds Cetti's Warbler and Nightingale. Rufous Bush Robin may frequently be found in summer lower down in the olive groves.

With care you can walk up the Gorge but the best views are normally to be had from the bridge itself.

Practical points

Much of the road south from Campillos is in the process of improvement at the time of writing, a process which looks set to continue for some years. This, though undoubtedly rendering the current boneshaker a little smoother, will be less than helpful to birders as stopping places seldom come high on the list of priorities with Spanish road builders and parking with your wheels on the road is illegal (and costly!).

There is ample accommodation in Ronda (Site D).

Bonelli's Eagle

Málage Site D: Ronda

Ronda is one of the principal tourist attractions of Andalucia. Its proximity to the beach resorts of Torremolinos and Marbella ensures a steady stream of coachloads of brightly- and often inadequately-clad tourists. This, however, does nothing to detract from the avian attractions of this amazing town. The old bridge (Punte Viejo) and the lookout (Mirador) both provide the unusual facility of seeing cliff-nesting species at very close hand and from above.

In the breeding season there are always Lesser Kestrels, often with Kestrel for comparison, Chough and Alpine Swift, as well as Blue Rock Thrush and Black Wheatear. Although they breed too, winter and early spring are better times to see Rock Sparrow and Peregrine. Pallid Swift join their common relatives over the town, too.

Sierras to the south are more than worthy of exploration and the valley of the Rio Guadiaro, to the southwest of the town, has a few herons and other water birds as well as frequent Wrens and Cetti's Warblers. Bridges may well have Red-rumped Swallows nesting beneath and their old nests have occasionally been taken over by the elusive White-rumped Swift in this region. The whole Serrañla de Ronda will replay a careful exploration if time permits.

Cork Oak woodland to the north of Ronda is especially rich in birdlife, with Woodlark, Mistle Thrush and Cirl Bunting, as well as tits, flycatchers and Jay.

Practical points

Ronda is no town to drive in! The best strategy is to park as soon as you can and walk.

The views into the gorge are vertiginous in the extreme, though good railings protect the viewpoints.

The number of hotels and restaurants is impressive and the scale of tourism actually helps main competition, forcing prices down rather than up.

The bullring is actually the oldest in Spain and they will tell you that in the bad old days when the horses didn't enjoy the protection they now have, they simply flung the ones that perished over the cliff for the vultures!

Murcia Province

Murcia is a large Province very diversified in character. It would be difficult to imagine sites more different than those of the Mar Menor with its ribbon development along tourist beaches and the wild mountains and plains in the west of the Province. The whole interior, in fact, away from the main towns is under-populated with an overwhelming impression of space and often a 'Spaghetti Western' type of scenery.

Agriculture is the main occupation of the inhabitants and, except along the coast, you will find little concession to tourism with almost no English spoken.

The climate is a harsh one with summer temperatures climbing to uncomfortable levels and a short, cold winter. Rainfall throughout is minimal, but flash floods can be brought about by the dreaded *'gota fria'* usually in autumn, a torrential downpour caused by warm air from the sea meeting cold air from the interior.

It is probably one of the least-visited Provinces of Spain and it is quite possible that ornithological discoveries can still be made there as there are few resident birders. There is certainly not the spectacular variety of raptors to be found further west, but there is a sufficient variety of birds to occupy a curious mind for a good few days.

Murcia: Site A: The Mar Menor and surroundings (Map 19)

Serious tourism-country this, and the summer months see thousands of holidaymakers ensconsed on the beaches, enjoying watersports and the like. Then, this is no place for the birder. However, in winter the waters of this massive 'inland sea' hold some concentrations of Black-necked Grebe and it is one of the few places along the Mediterranean coast where you can find Red-breasted Merganser (up to 200 birds).

A few pairs of Shelduck breed and there is a nice area of 'steppe' land near Las Urrútias which is reliable for Calandra Lark and Quail (you can LISTEN to them anyway!) in spring and Stone Curlew and Lesser Short-toed Lark can also be found.

Map 19. The Mer Menor and surrounding area.

48

Calandra Lark

The salinas to the north (San Pedro del Pínatar) and to the south (Cabo de Palos) are worth a look and can be good for waders at passage times.

Some of the offshore islets you will see on the map (outside the 'inland sea') support small populations of Storm Petrel and a few pairs of Cory's Shearwaters, but the presence of rats on at least one of them has wiped out both species.

Sea-watching from the Cabo de Palos can be quite rewarding, especially in strong winds, but you may find it easy to resist a trip along 'La Manga' (it means 'the sleeve') which is nothing more than a concrete jungle of hotels and apartments.

Practical points

Access to any of the sites, other than the islets mentioned above, is no problem but peak holiday times are to be avoided at all costs. There is ample accommodation in the area at other times, with apartments aplenty just to the north in Torrevieja from where you could explore the sites of Alicante Province (see 'Birdwatching Guide to 'Eastern Spain', Arlequin Press). Hotels and Motels abound along the main coast road and there are lots of campsites too.

Access to the offshore islets would have to be by private boat and should, in any case, be avoided during the breeding season as the birds have enough to contend with as it is.

Murcia: Site B: The Sierras of Cartagena (Map 19)

There are persistent rumours of Trumpeter Finch colonising these low mountains and there exists some excellent habitat for that species, but they are extremely difficult to find here and you may well be advised to seek that species further south in Almería Province where they are undoubtedly more numerous. However, the hills are of more than passing ornithological interest and will repay a morning's visit, at least. The eastern end has disused salinas and is the site where the elusive Trumpeters have been seen in the past. Two or three pairs of Bonelli's Eagles, a similar number of Peregrines and a few Ravens are resident and at passage times the whole area can heave with vast migrants.

Practical points

The western end of the sierra, despite what other guides may tell you, is one vast petro-chemical installation and definitely best avoided.

Some of the access roads marked at the eastern end are dodgy, especially after heavy rain when they may be impassable. The village of Portman is a curiosity, probably not to be dwelt upon for long, as it is nothing more than an abandoned mining village with an eerie air of dereliction. La Union resembles nowhere more closely than Merthyr

Tydfil! — and I do not flatter the 'valleys' by that comparison! For accommodation refer to Site A.

Murcia: Site C: Plains of Alcanara (Map 20)

This is a site which is the vestigial remains of a once-huge tract of lowland salt steppe occupying the valley of the largely dried-up Guadalentin. Here is the best site in Murcia Province for Black-bellied Sandgrouse. Given decent weather and a lack of hunting activity they are reliable here and you will have a good chance of Little Bustard, Stone Curlew and a good variety of larks. Both Short-toed species are here in summer and Lesser throughout the year. Little Bustard are most likely in winter, but may be found at any time. It is also a good place for raptors, particularly Montagu's Harrier in summer. Spectacled Warbler and Black-eared Wheatear breed commonly and Rollers are numerous, especially near to the river course. They may be parasitised by Great Spotted Cuckoo which you can often see here too.

Practical points

Do not attempt to traverse the earth tracks across the area after rain, as the mud will soon bring you to a sticky end. Just occasionally the military use the area for exercises. If they are (they have been twice out of about fifty visits for me), you will be lucky to see anything. In hot weather heat-haze can make birding tough going after about eleven o'clock. The best system by far is to drive around the innumerable tracks ready to leap out if you put something up. There are also little reservoirs dotted around. They occasionally harbour thirsty birds and their banks also make good vantage points. For some reason the whole area is plagued by flies which can be remarkably irritating and the dust can also be a nuisance, especially if you leave the car windows open when another vehicle passes.

There is a plethora of hotels along the excellent motorway which passes close by the site.

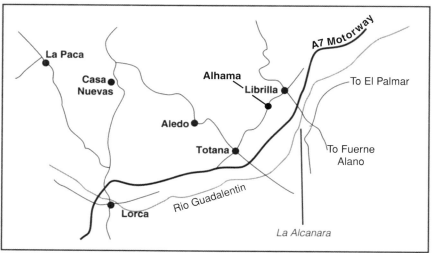

Map 20. Plains of Alcanara.

Murcia: Site D: Sierra Espuña (Map 21)

This relatively isolated little mountain range reaches up to about 1,500 metres in height and is home to the usual range of montane species found in the south of Spain, including Crossbills, Rock Bunting, Short-toed Treecreeper, Crested Tit and some 'English' things

50

Map 21. Sierra Espuña.

like Mistle Thrush, Wren and Jay. Mammal buffs will be interested in the endemic race of Red Squirrel as well as the charming Mouflon and the plentiful Wild Boar. There are two or three good cliffs which, rock-climbers permitting, sport Golden Eagle, Peregrine, Alpine Swift and Chough, whilst Booted Eagle and Eagle Owl are not uncommon in the well-forested mountains. An isolated population of the elusive Dupont's Lark is to be found in one area.

Practical points

The road which traverses the Sierra is slow going with many hairpin bends as well as some spectacular drops into the valley. For those of a nervous disposition it may be worth avoiding. The tracks marked, especially to the 'Red Cliff', are rough and stony, more suitable to all-terrain vehicles.

There are two or three bars in the park itself and several good restaurants in the neighbourhood of Aledo. One such may be recommended, the 'Finca Caruan', which also has chalet-style accommodation at reasonable prices. This is close to the Dupont's Lark site at which it is necessary to present yourself at dawn or dusk to have a chance of hearing them in song. The area is one of wild beauty and little human population.

Murcia: Site E: Alfonso XIII (Map 22)

The reservoir bearing that king's name lies deep in wild country between the towns of Cieza and Calasparra. Although parts of it look deep and hold little but the odd Great Crested Grebe, there are sizeable reedbeds which can be full of birds during spring migration. The cliffs near the dam are very impressive and Golden and Bonelli's Eagle nest, as do Peregrine and Chough (sparingly). Goshawk are in the pinewoods nearby and you can also see the usual Crag Martins, Black Wheatear and Blue Rock Thrush.

To the southwest of the reservoir, bordering the MU-552 road, are extensive cereal fields. In the period when crops are growing to optimum height this area holds a substantial population of Black-bellied Sandgrouse, a few Little Bustards and plenty of Stone Curlews. Rock Sparrows are often around the outcrops in this area.

Practical points

The road around the reservoir is quite good, but requires care and is limited (by a tunnel) to vehicles not exceeding 3.3 metres in height.

On the agricultural plains there are lots of farm tracks. Caution, as ever, should be exercised here. In an area as remote as this, a mechanical failure or accident could be embarrassing.

There are hotels, restaurants and bars in all the towns of the area, more particularly in Mula and Archena, which have hot springs.

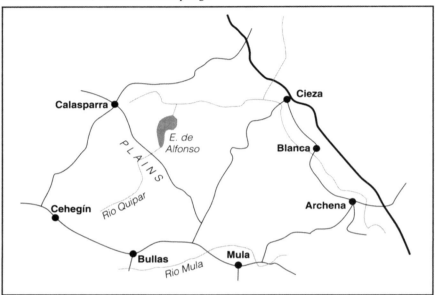

Map 22. Alfonso XIII reservoir.

Murcia: Site F: The plains of Tornajuelo (Map 23)

This is a real 'Extremadura-type' plain, stretching away to the south of the fast road from Caravaca westwards into Andalucia. Many of the tracks and even metalled roads which criss-cross this vast area do not find their way onto maps and you should devote a good few hours to exploration if you mean to get the best out of the area.

The little river valleys and the neighbourhood of the tiny hamlets often have some very marginal-looking agriculture and these areas often turn up little flocks of Rock Sparrow as well as Rollers. The area has many raptors, especially in spring and a carcase left out somewhere will inevitably bring flocks of Griffon Vultures around. Peregrines and Booted Eagles, as well as Montagu's Harrier, are frequent. This is probably the last place in southeast Spain to have a population (a few pairs only) of Pin-tailed Sandgrouse, whilst Black-bellied Sandgrouse and Little Bustard are relatively numerous.

Practical points

Heat-haze can be a problem here and the heat in midsummer can be extreme. 'Early or late' seems to be the best advice here, in consequence. There is no accommodation to speak of in the area, but Puebla de Don Fadrique has a Pension and I can personally vouch for the Hotel Ruta del Sur a little further south in Huescar. Both the last-named towns are in Granada Province.

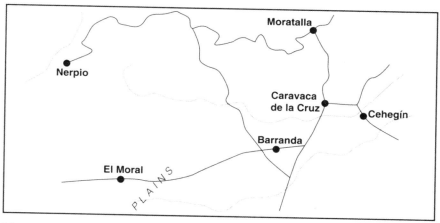

Map 23. The Plains of Tornajuelo.

Murcia: Site G: Sierra de Moratalla

This site lies in the wildest country on the borders of Murcia and Albacete Provinces. It is an important breeding area for Bonelli's Eagle (5 pairs), Golden Eagle (7), Peregrine (18) and Eagle Owl (15+). In addition, there Chough, Raven and Carrion Crow — an oddly rare species in southern Spain. The country is arid with rolling hills, sparse agriculture and some pretty basic villages. The rocky outcrops are often worth a look with flocks of Rock Sparrow always a possibility, though never, seemingly, in the same place twice!

Practical points

A very lonely, isolated area, this. Make sure you have petrol and something to drink before you embark on the minor roads here.

Accommodation: see previous site.

Pintailed Sandgrouse

Out of area sites
Ciudad Real

Although not part of Andalucía (this is a Province of Castilla-la Mancha) the one area covered here is of particular interest and could well be incorporated into the itinerary, especially if you are making your way northwards, say to Madrid.

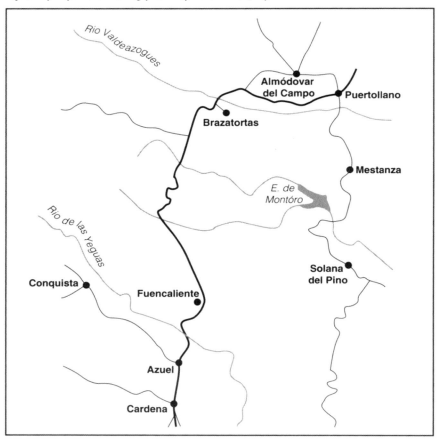

Map 24. Sierra de Mórena, raptor country.

Fuencaliente/Alcúdia

The Sierra de Morena reaches its wildest and rockiest point here around Fuencaliente. Much is wooded, often with dense, tall oaks but there are areas of 'dehesa' and more of scrub.

Almost all of the raptors of Spain occur here, including Black-shouldered Kite, Imperial Eagle, Red Kite and Goshawk. Passerines too abound and mammals are represented by virtually all the larger species still to be found in Spain including Wolf and Lynx.

All the way from Fuencaliente northwards to and just beyond the highest point of the pass, the Puerto de Niefla (908m), you are passing through wild, well-wooded country and raptors as well as Black Stork pass overhead with some regularity.

Further north the road drops into the Valley of Alcúdia and you find yourself in steppe-like country, with an excellent chance of Stone Curlew, Little Bustard and larks, including Calandra and Short-toed. Cranes winter here as do Great Bustard. A diversion westwards towards Bienvenida may also be worthwhile.

Practical points

Plenty of time — and petrol — should be allowed for viewing this wild country.

Fuencaliente has a range of hotels you may find surprising, until you realise that the name means 'hot spring' — it is a spa town.

Puertollano to the north has more.

Great Bustard

Ackowledgements

In writing a book at this kind, it is inevitable that other guides are referred to from time to time, even if only to check for points of divergence and/or agreement. The works of de Juana/SEO and Patterson and Garcia have been consulted frequently, as have several official publications issued by Provincial and Regional authorities.

However, the vast bulk of this guide is a result of personal fieldwork, undertaken on a great number of occasions, over a period of several years.

For assistance in this enterprise, I owe grateful thanks to a wide variety of clients of my company Calandra Holidays and to too many colleagues to mention individually.

My species list follows, in general, that of Voous 1977 (List of Recent Holarctic Bird Species) and the names used are those in normal usage at the time of writing. I still retain a fancy for 'Rufous Bush Chat', but the bird's song strikes me as sufficiently Robin-like to sway me in that direction, hence 'Rufous Bush Robin'.

My grateful thanks are due to Juana Martinez Garcia for her encouragement and unfailing optimism, to Luis Fidel for his many offers of help and to Lynn Palmer for invaluable assistance with the drafts. A great deal of initial assistance with Murcia Province was provided by Jose Damian Navarro Medina.

Bibliography

Cramp et al: Birds of the Western Palearctic — OUP
De Juana/SEO: Areas Importantes para las Aves en España — SEO
                    Donde ver Aves en España Peninsular — Lynx
Garcia/Patterson: Where to Watch Birds in Southern Spain — Christopher Helm
Grimmett/Jones/IWRB/RSPB: Important Bird Areas in Europe — ICBP
Junta de Andalucía: Various local publications on reserves*

* These most useful little booklets are often handed out by wardens at the various sites and worth keeping your eye out for. Although they are invariably in Spanish they will usually contain useful access information, maps, etc. They are hard to keep track of, but a recent pbulication on the Lagoons of Cádiz is accurate and useful. A request to the Agencia de Medio Ambiente, Ana de Villa, 3.3o, 11009 Cádiz, may bear fruit.

Booted Eagle

Specific List and Brief Habitat Guide

NB: This list is limited to those species which occur, or have occurred, regularly in the region covered.

Seabirds of mainly Atlantic distribution have only been included if fairly common, as the potential list is enormous, and it is believed that the users of this guide will normally prefer to concentrate on more terrestrial species.

Red-throated Diver *Gavia stellata*
A scarce but regular winter visitor to any coast, more likely off Atlantic shores.

Little Grebe *Tachybaptus ruficollis*
Common but local breeding species, on deeper waters. Very numerous in winter, including offshore.

Great Crested Grebe *Podiceps cristatus*
Common but local breeding species, on deeper waters. Very numerous in winter, including offshore.

Black-necked Grebe *Podiceps nigricollis*
Breeds on many lagoons throughout Andalucia. Big numbers occur in winter, especially on sheltered inlets such as the Mar Menor.

Cory's Shearwater *Calonectris diomedea*
Movements of sometimes large numbers of this species may be seen from prominent headlands in spring and autumn, especially through the Straits, and from the Cabo de Gata, for instance.

Mediterranean Shearwater *Puffinus yellkouan*
A common offshore species often gathering in rafts wherever fish concentrations are high. Breeds on some islets off the Murcia coasts.

Storm Petrel *Hydrobates pelagicus*
Most likely to be seen from ships crossing the Straits, etc. Breeds in small numbers on a few islets.

Gannet *Sula bassana*
A surprisingly common sight from almost any headland, at most times of year, though only a few non-breeders to be found in summer.

Cormorant *Phalacrocorax carbo*
An abundant winter visitor to larger inland waters,

Shag *Phalacrocorax aristoteles*
May still breed at Gibraltar, and just possibly on the coast of Almería and around Cartagena. A scarce vagrant elsewhere.

Bittern *Botaurus stellaris*
A rare winter visitor, which has, however, bred historically in the Coto Doñana.

Little Bittern *Ixobrychus minutus*
Common summer visitor. A few stay to winter, especially in the southeast. Is restricted to reedbeds and reed-filled dykes.

Night Heron *Nycticorax nycticorax*
Summer visitor and passage migrant, breeding in colonies, often with other herons. Some stay on to winter. Can be retiring and hard to find, especially away from colonies.

Cattle Egret *Bubulcus ibis*
A common and conspicuous resident, forming massive colonies, and not always requiring the presence of cattle — a tractor (or a rubbish dump) will do!

Squacco Heron *Ardeola ralloides*
Summer visitor in small numbers. Late April to October. Reedbeds and also quite insignificant ponds and ditches.

Little Egret

Little Egret *Egretta garzetta*
Summer visitor, winter visitor, passage migrant and resident, abundant around major wetland sites, often quite absent elsewhere.

Grey Heron *Ardea cinerea*
Nests in the Coto Doñana, and possibly in Almería. Huge numbers winter at many sites.

Purple Heron *Ardea purpurea*
A common summer visitor to almost any reedbed, often arriving in early April and departing in October.

Black Stork *Ciconia nigra*
A scarce breeding bird, which occasionally winters. Breeds on rocky ledges and in caves in the northwest of the region, and is usually present from March to October. During passage times may join in with movements of the next species, especially across the Straits.

White Stork *Ciconia ciconia*
Very common as a breeding species in the west of our region. Some also stay on to winter around the towns and villages. Big movements occur across the Straits, August being the best month for southwards passage.

Glossy Ibis *Plegadis falcinellus*
Probably breeds in Huelva Province. Occasional elsewhere, especially in winter. Another denizen of reedbeds.

Spoonbill *Platalea leucorodia*
Breeds Coto Doñana and further west, and may occur at almost any suitable wetland during winter and spring wanderings.

Greater Flamingo *Phoenicopterus ruber*
The only regular breeding site at the time of writing is the Fuente de Piedra, but has bred historically in the Coto Doñana. May occur at almost any largish wetland, and is present all year at such sites as the Cabo de Gata. Many Camargue birds disperse southwards and turn up, at almost any time, along the east coast of Spain, when their colour-rings may be quite easily read with a telescope.

Greylag Goose *Anser anser*
Winters in big numbers at the Coto Doñana. Accidental elsewhere.

Ruddy Shelduck *Tadorna ferruginea*
Probably bred in relatively recent times in an around Doñana, but now an irregular visitor from north Africa, where a small breeding population still exists.

Shelduck *Tadorna tadorna*
Breeds around the Mar Menor, and possibly in Doñana, where it is a common winter visitor in large numbers (hundreds).

Wigeon *Anas penelope*
Common winter visitor to all major waters.

Gadwall *Anas strepera*
Good numbers breed on the Jaén reservoirs, and may be met with almost anywhere. Augmented in winter by numbers from further north.

Teal *Anas crecca*
Common in winter on Doñana, but quite shy and retiring, especially where shooting is prevalent.

Mallard *Anas platyrhynchos*
Common breeder and winter visitor.

Pintail *Anas acuta*
Winter visitor to sites like the Coto Doñana and the Laguna de Medina, often forming large flocks on open water.

Garganey *Anas querquedula*
A scarce passage migrant, especially in spring, when males appear to predominate — usually in small flocks. February and March.

Shoveler *Anas clypeata*
A scarce breeding bird and abundant winter visitor, some sites having numbers of many thousands.

Marbled Duck *Marmaronetta angustirostris*
Scarce but widespread breeding visitor to small reedy lagoons. Some stay to winter, and in autumn they may be much more easily seen, frequenting larger waters, and forming flocks.

Red-crested Pochard *Netta ruffina*
Breeds commonly on lagooons throughout. Winters in good flocks.

Pochard *Aythya ferina*
As Shoveler, but wintering numbers slightly smaller.

Ferruginous Duck *Aythya nyroca*
A very local and unpredictable species, breeding on small reedy ponds, but perhaps more likely to be seen as a rare visitor to larger waters outside the nesting season.

Tufted Duck *Aythya fuligula*
Not nearly so numerous as Pochard but common in winter.

Common Scoter *Melanitta negra*
A common wintering species, mainly off Atlantic coasts, but also found in smaller flocks in the Mediterranean.

Red-breasted Merganser *Mergus serrator*
May be found off any coasts during the winter months, usually in ones and twos, but larger gatherings may occur, especially in the Mar Menor and off Cádiz.

Ruddy Duck *Oxyura jamaicensis*
A polemic situation has surfaced around this species in recent years as birds from preseumably British feral stocks have infiltrated some of the haunts of the next species. Hybridisation has been recorded at several sites and the authorities have started an extermination programme. This raises questions as to the specific status of both, of course, and the eventual outcome is far from clear. At the time of writing numbers of Ruddy Duck appear to be fairly small.

White-headed Duck *Oxyura leucocephala*
From a very tiny breeding population as recently as the 1960s, when they were restricted to a very few pairs, mainly in the Cádiz lagoons, the population has increased dramatically in recent years, with the main centre of population shifting in the 1990s to the coastal lagoons of Almería. Still, however, found in Cádiz and Doñana, as well as some of the Córdoba lagoons. Favours small reedy ponds for breeding, but as with other wildfowl, prefers larger waters in winter.

Honey Buzzard *Pernis apivorus*
Common and spectacular passage migrant over the Straits in May and September when many thousands pass. Strong westerly winds often displace this species far to the east of their normal route.

Black-shouldered Kite *Elanus caeruleus*
Most likely to be met with, usually in pairs or singly, in the dehesa country of Northern Córdoba or Sevilla and around Doñana. Wanders away from these areas in winter.

Red Kite

Black Kite *Milvus migrans*
An abundant passage migrant across the Straits, mainly in March/April and August/September. Breeds commonly in the Doñana area and many other parts of the west of the region.

Red Kite *Milvus milvus*
Much commoner in winter when the previous species is almost entirely absent, but breeds sparingly in rolling wooded country.

Lammergeier *Gypaetus barbatus*
Formerly bred in the Sierra de Cazoria where there were five pairs as late as the 1950s. There are now plans to reintroduce the species from Greek stock at the same site.

Egyptian Vulture *Neophron percnopterus*
Now becoming scarcer than it used to be, but still nesting on cliffs in the Sierras. Migrants are seen annually crossing the Straits, normally no more than a few hundred, in March/April and September.

Griffon Vulture *Gyps fulvus*
A common resident of almost all sierras which offer suitable cliff faces. Frequents rubbish tips. Winter flocks may run into hundreds.

Black Vulture *Aegypius monachus*
A tree-nesting species, this largest European raptor favours the wooded Sierras like Andújar and Morena. Resident, wandering far away from breeding sites in the winter.

Short-toed Eagle *Circaetus gallicus*
Fairly common as a breeding species, frequenting bare, rocky hills. A common passage migrant in March and September over the Straits. Many pass along the Sierra de Cazoria in early April.

Marsh Harrier *Circus aeruginosus*
A scarce breeding species and common winter visitor, passage birds can cause confusion when seen from below. Beware!

Hen Harrier *Circus cyaneus*
A common winter visitor to steppe and agricultural land throughout.

Montagu's Harrier *Circus pygargus*
A common breeding species and passage migrant, frequently seen hunting over cereal crops in all parts of the region.

Goshawk *Accipiter gentilis*
A numerous breeding species in all suitable wooded hills, but shy and retiring here as elsewhere.

Sparrowhawk *Accipiter nisus*
Much as last species, though more given to winter wanderings and many cross the Straits in spring and autumn.

Buzzard *Buteo buteo*
Common resident in open country, numbers being augmented in winter by birds from further north

Imperial Eagle *Aquila heliaca*
The Spanish race *A. adelberti* is probably at its greatest density in the Coto Doñana where some 4 pairs nest. Also found in wooded sierras, notably Andújar and Morena. A tree-nesting species requiring large tracts of woodland and a ready supply of rabbits, it may be increasing slowly under considerable protection.

Golden Eagle *Aquila chrysaetos*
Resident in most of the region, wandering over the plains to feed.

Booted Eagle *Hieraatus pennatus*
A common sight crossing the Strait in March and April and coursing along north-south mountain ranges on both passages. Breeds in wooded hills throughout the region with an increasing tendency to overwinter.

Bonelli's Eagle *Hieraatus fasciatus*
A resident of cliff faces wherever suitable ones are found. Seldom wanders far from its home range and may spend hours of inactivity on a perch there.

Osprey *Pandion halieetus*
Winter visitor to regular sites in many areas and passage migrant.

Lesser Kestrel *Falco naumanni*
Colonies are found in towns and villages and on natural rock faces throughout Western Andalucía, despite a huge general decline. Some birds winter and new colonies are apt to crop up anywhere including Murcia, when they may be occupied as early as January.

Kestrel *Falco tinnunculs*
Common and widespread.

Merlin *Falco columbarius*
A common winter visitor, hunting over reedbeds and in rocky gorges and ravines as well as open steppes.

Hobby *Falco subbuteo*
A surprisingly scarce summer visitor and regular passage migrant often staying late into October and even November.

Peregrine *Falco peregrinus*
Common breeding species of rock faces everywhere.

Red-legged Partridge *Alectoris rufa*
Common, though often crepuscular species, in almost all habitats.

Quail *Coturnix coturnix*
Common though often unseen summer visitor and occasional wintering species.

Pheasant *Phasianus colchicus*
A few are shot in various areas, notably in Cádiz Province.

Andalucian Hemipode *Turnix sylvatica*
No! The writer has only ever met one birder who has reliably seen one in Spain! Coastal scrub in Huelva Province was the site of that momentous find and a tiny population may still be there. If you see one, tell me.

Water Rail *Rallus aquaticus*
Common resident and very common winter visitor to waterside vegetation.

Spotted Crake *Porzana porzana*
Breeds in some reedy wetlands, notably Doñana and winters widely, also passing through on both journeys.

Little Crake *Porzana parva*
Breeds in the Coto, but incompletely known, for obvious reasons.

Baillon's Crake *Porzana pusilla*
As last species, but not even really known to nest.

Moorhen *Gallinula chloropus*
Back to reality! Common everywhere.

Purple Gallinule *Porphyrio porphyrio*
Spreading fairly rapidly, colonising ever further north and east and at home in reedbeds alongside lakes and rivers. The Guadalquivir valley is probably the centre of the population.

Coot *Fulica atra*
Abundant in winter on all waters, many also staying to breed.

Crested Coot *Fulica cristata*
The Cádiz lagoons and Doñana are almost certainly the only places where you will find this rare species, though odd ones have turned up in many other places in recent years of drought. Not usually seen consorting with the last species, which is a help!

Crane *Grus grus*
Apart from overflying flocks at passage times, best looked for in winter in dehesa country in Western Andalucia.

Great Bustard *Otis tarda*
Only likely in Northern Córdoba where winter flocks may be in crops and the odd pair still breeds. A few may still appear in winter at other sites, notably La Janda.

Little Bustard *Tetrax tetrax*
Locally common in grasslands and crops, which it tolerates readily. Small number occur in many parts of the eastern regions and greater numbers in the west.

Oystercatcher *Haematopus ostralogus*
Coastal passage migrant and winter visitor, never very common.

Black-winged Stilt

Black-winged Stilt *Himantopusd himantopus*
Common resident, withdrawing from the colder areas in hard weather.

Avocet *Recurvirostra avisetta*
Big numbers occur in winter throughout the coastal areas. Breeds in small numbers in many parts.

Stone Curlew *Burhinus oedicnemus*
Moderately common in steppes and rough open country, though a nocturnal visit is necessary to really assess for species' status in any area. Large flocks winter in many, usually coastal, sites.

Cream-coloured Courser *Cursorius cursor*
Recently discovered breeding in a remote area in Southeast Spain, at least eleven birds being present throughout the summer, and four pairs successfully raising young.

Collared Pratincole *Glareola pratincola*
Summer visitor, first turning up in late March and becoming common and widespread by May on dry mudflats and saltmarsh. A few may stay on into September.

Little Ringed Plover *Charadrius dubius*
Breeds very sparingly along rivers in their region. Winters fairly regularly and is common passage.

Ringed Plover *Charadrius hiaticula*
Common passage migrant and winter visitor, usually on coasts.

Kentish Plover *Charadrius alexandrinus*
Common breeding species of sandy shores, passage migrant and winter visitor.

Golden Plover *Pluvialis apricarius*
Winter visitor to steppe and stubble fields, usually in small numbers.

Grey Plover *Pluvialis squaterola*
Common passage migrant and winter visitor, a few individuals summering.

Lapwing *Vanellus vanellus*
A very few birds breed in the western area, but largely a winter visitor, often in large numbers.

Knot *Calidris canutus*
Scarce passage migrant, most often seen in May and August/September.

Sanderling *Calidris alba*
Passage migrant visitor and passage migrant.

Little Stint *Calidris temminckii*
Very scarce, though regular, passage migrant and rare winter visitor to more freshwater sites than the last species.

Temminck's Stint *Calidris temminckii*
Very scarce, though regular, passage migrant and rare winter visitor to more freshwater sites than the last species.

Curlew Sandpiper *Calidris ferruginea*
Common migrant and rare winter visitor. Flocks of several hundred may form at favoured sites.

Purple Sandpiper *Calidris maritima*
Rare but regular winter visitor to rocky coasts.

Dunlin *Calidris alpina*
Common migrant and winter visitor.

Ruff *Philomachus pugnax*
Common on passage at freshwater marshes. Less so in winter.

Jack Snipe *Lymnocryptes minimus*
Many winter in Doñana and smaller numbers in marshes elsewhere.

Snipe *Gallinago gallinago*
Abundant winter visitor to all suitable sites.

Woodcock *Glareola pratincola*
Winter visitor to coastal marshes and dunes in sizeable numbers.

Black-tailed Godwit *Limosa limosa*
Common winter visitor and passage migrant, often forming large flocks on saltpans and shallow waters

Bar-tailed Godwit *Limosa lapponica*
Nowhere as numerous as the last species. Largely a late spring and autumn migrant, though small numbers winter on coast of Cádiz and probably elsewhere.

Whimbrel *Numenius phaeopus*
Common migrant and wintering species in small numbers, often on shorelines.

Curlew *Numenius arquata*
Probably scarcer generally than last species but regular on passage and in winter.

Spotted Redshank *Tringa erythropus*
Common passage migrant and winter visitor to many marshes.

Redshank *Tringa totanus*
Breeding species in small numbers and abundant winter visitor.

Marsh Sandpiper *Tringa stagnatilis*
Regular passage migrant in very small numbers, usually to fresh marshes, a few winter in Doñana and elsewhere.

Greenshank *Tringa nebularia*
Largely as Spotted Redshank with which it is frequently to be seen.

Green Sandpiper *Tringa ochropus*
Regular winter visitor to dykes and ditches and common migrant.

Wood Sandpiper *Tringa glareola*
Common migrant and winter visitor in much smaller numbers. Usually on fresh marshes.

Common Sandpiper *Actitis hypoleucos*
Breeds on some mountain streams and possibly around a few of the upland reservoirs. Otherwise a common migrant and increasing winter visitor.

Turnstone *Arenaria interpres*
Regular passage migrant turning up almost anywhere in small numbers.

Red-necked Phalarope *Phalaropus lobatus*
An occasional passage visitor to coastal areas.

Grey Phalarope *Phalaropus fulicarius*
An occasional visitor to coastal locations usually in winter.

Pomarine Skua *Stercorarius pomarinus*
Regular coastal migrant in very small numbers, spring and autumn.

Arctic Skua *Stercorarius parasiticus*
Common migrant on both passages with some birds remaining to winter.

Great Skua *Stercorarius skua*
As last species, but probably scarcer.

Mediterranean Gull *Larus melanocephalus*
An unpredictable migrant which can be met with at almost any season, usually on the coast.

Little Gull *Larus minutus*
Much as last species, but more likely to be seen on inland waters, especially in late spring.

Black-headed Gull *Larus ridibundus*
Abundant as a winter visitor and passage migrant. Some breeding colonies exist at widely scattered localities.

Slender-billed Gull *Larus geneii*
Colonies exist in Doñana and occasionally at Fuente de Piedra. There is also a chance of breeding around the Mar Menor, but this species fluctuates with water levels and other factors. Generally on the increase, but slowly. Almost always found where there is saline, shallow water.

Audouin's Gull *Larus audouini*
Common migrant along Mediterranean coasts. Big numbers roost at various points on the coasts of Almería and Murcia, usually in the vicinity of salt pans and birds may be found there in any month, but the biggest concentrations tend to be in late summer when numbers at Cabo de Gata Salinas, for instance, may run to 500+.

Lesser Black-backed Gull *Larus fuscus*
Common winter vistor to all coasts.

Great Black-backed Gull *Larus marinus*
Winters in very small numbers off the Atlantic coast - rare elsewhere.

Yellow-legged Gull *Larus cachinnans*
Common resident at many points along the coast, especially around fishing ports and where rocky coastlines offer breeding sites.

Kittiwake *Rissa tridactyla*
A winter visitor mainly to the Atlantic coast.

Gull-billed Tern *Gelochelidon nilotica*
A few colonies are to be found in the region, particularly in Doñana, where parties of 30-40 may be seen feeding, often over fields. Fuenta de Fiedra usually has a small colony too. Also an occasional passage bird on the east coast, particularly at the Mar Menor and Almería.

Caspian Tern *Sterna caspia*
Passage migrant and winter visitor in small numbers, often seen offshore and over salt pans.

Lesser Crested Tern *Sterna bengalensis*
Seen annually along the coast often in the company of Sandwich Terns and in May and October. On the increase and now breeding to the north of our region in Valencia. Probably a good candidate for breeding here too.

Sandwich Tern *Sterna sandvicensis*
Common passage migrant and winter visitor to coasts.

Common Tern *Sterna hirundo*
Breeds occasionally Doñana and also near the Mar Menor. Otherwise is a common passage migrant and occasional winter visitor.

Little Tern *Sterna albifrons*
Breeds in good numbers on the Atlantic shore and also around the Mar Menor and the Almería coast.

Whiskered Tern *Chlidonias hybridus*
Common breeding species in Doñana and particularly at some inland lagoons such as Puerto Real. Very local elsewhere. A few winter in Doñana.

Black Tern *Chlidonias niger*
May breed Doñana and possibly at a few lagoons, but rather scarce generally except for coastal passage migrants in May and September.

White-winged Black Tern *Chlidonias leucopterus*
A regular visitor after easterly winds in April and May. Rarer in autumn.

Razorbill *Alca torda*
Regular winter visitor to all coasts from which it is often easily seen.

Puffin *Fratercula arctica*
Regular on passage through the Straits in last autumn and early spring.

Black-bellied Sandgrouse *Pterocles orientalis*
A classic 'steppe' species frequenting exclusively uncultivated flat land, usually with *Salicorna* and *Esparto*. Locally common in Almería and Murcia and also on the Hoya de Guadix.

Pin-tailed Sandgrouse *Pterocles alchata*
Found in habitats similar to the last species, though possibly less stony ground. Found around the Coto Doñana where suitable steppe may still exit. A small relic population exists in Murcia too, but not found in Almería.

Rock Dove *Columba livia*
Tick them if you like! The more remote coastal localities have some convincing-looking ones, until you find the multi-coloured associate.

Stock Dove *Columba oenas*
Scarce resident of wooded ranges and commoner winter visitor.

Woodpigeon *Columba palumbas*
Common breeding species and abundant winter visitor.

Collared Dove *Streptopelia decaocto*
Locally common and spreading where colonisation has taken place, such as Totana, Murcia and along the coast of Malaga, Mercifully scarce elsewhere. Because the closely-related Barbary Dove which is feral at some sites — and, presumably, even stands a chance of reaching the region unaided from Africa

*Great
Spotted Cuckoo*

Turtle Dove *Streptopelia turtur*
Common summer visitor and migrant.

Great Spotted Cuckoo: Roller *Clamator Glandarius*
Parasitic upon Magpie, Azure-winged Magpie and roller (and possibly Jay) in the region, so only worth looking for where these species occur, in the breeding season. A good many overwinter, probably having carried out their migration south at the end of the nesting season and returned already. Often seen in steppe country.

Cuckoo *Cuculus canorus*
Common summer visitor and passage migrant.

Barn Owl *Tyto alba*
Common resident.
Scops Owl *Otus scops*
Common summer visitor to parks and gardens usually with pines. Strictly nocturnal, singing best in April. A few overwinter.

Eagle Owl *Bubo bubo*
Quite common in dry river valleys, wooded gorges and cliffs. The necessary combination consists of suitable caves for nesting and a supply of rabbits or rats. Often found near rubbish tips, but very nocturnal.

Little Owl *Athene noctua*
Common resident in many habitats.

Tawny Owl *Strix aluco*
Widespread and locally common in woodland.

Long-eared Owl *Asio otus*
Resident of mature pine woods.

Short-eared Owl *Asio flammeus*
Passage migrant and winter visitor, in small and variable numbers.

Nightjar *Caprimulgus europaeus*
Summer resident of upland heaths, but very local. Also passage migrant.
Red-necked Nightjar *Caprimulgus ruficollis*
Commoner than last species preferring more wooded habitat. Does not usually appear until late April. Very nocturnal, usually singing from half-an-hour after sunset.

Swift *Apus apus*
Abundant summer visitor with odd records in winter. Does not normally arrive until a full month after the next species and departs much earlier.

Pallid Swift *Apus pallidus*
Locally common summer visitor arriving in early March and departing in October. Mainly coastal in distribution and normally on natural cliffs.
Alpine Swift *Apus melba*
Common colonial breeder appearing at about the same date as the last species. Nests on cliffs and rockfaces.

White-rumped Swift *Apus caffer*
A summer visitor in small numbers using old nests of Red-rumped Swallow. On the increase, but still most likely to be found in the southernmost sierras of Cádiz Province.

Kingfisher *Alcedo atthis*
Winter visitor to lowland wetlands and the coast. Breeds locally on mountain streams.

Bee Eater *Merops apiaster*
Common colonial breeding species, needing sandy banks in which to nest and arriving in late March, staying into September.

Roller *Coracias garrulus*
Uncommon breeding species, preferring steppe terrain with lookout posts and breeding holes. Will take to nestboxes. Locally more common in Murcia and northern Córdoba.

Hoopoe

Hoopoe *Upopa epops*
Common breeding bird in many types of habitat. Large numbers winter in coastal localities.

Wryneck *Jynx torquilla*
Breeds locally in open woodland. Winters in reedbeds near the coast in small numbers.

Green Woodpecker *Picus viridis*
The Iberian race is moderately common as a resident.

Great Spotted Woodpecker *Dendrocopus major*
Common breeding resident of mature woodland, particularly coniferous. Absent from some apparently suitable areas, particularly in the east.

Lesser Spotted Woodpecker *Dendrocopus minor*
Scarce and local in deciduous woodland in Jaén Province.

Dupont's Lark *Chersophilis duponti*
Uncommon resident of flat uncultivated plains with *Esparto* cover, in Murcia, Almería and Granada Provinces. Sings only at dawn and dusk and is very hard to flush. A vehicle will help on occasion.

Calandra Lark *Melanocorypha calandra*
Locally common on cultivated plains, flocking in winter.

Short-toed Lark *Calandrella brachydactyla*
Common summer visitor to stony ground, usually arriving in April and staying to September.

Lesser Short-toed Lark *Calandra rufescens*
A resident of salt flats, occasionally found alongside the previous species. Confined to lowland sites in Almería and Murcia and around Doñana.

Crested Lark *Galerida cristata*
Resident of agricultural and suburban country.

Thekla Lark

Thekla Lark *Galerida thekiae*
Takes the place of the last species in mountains and rocky ground.

Woodlark *Lullula arborea*
Common breeding bird of upland woods throughout.

Skylark *Alauda arvensis*
Breeds at high altitude in the Sierra Nevada, otherwise a common winter visitor, sometimes in big flocks.

Sand Martin *Riparia riparia*
Common passage migrant staying to breed in suitable places.

Crag Martin *Ptyonoprogne rupestris*
Breeding species at many suitable cliffs. Winters at lower levels, often forming huge flocks over water.

Swallow *Hirundo rustica*
Abundant summer resident and increasing wintering species.

Red-rumped Swallow *Hirundo daurica*
Often a very early spring migrant. Locally common summer visitor and passage bird. Nests under bridges.

House Martin *Delichon urbica*
Abundant summer visitor arriving in February and showing an increasing tendency to winter in small numbers.

Tawny Pipit *Anthus campestris*
Summer visitor to upland plains and bare mountain areas, local in the region.

Tree Pipit *Anthus trivialis*
A characteristic passage migrant in March or September.

Meadow Pipit *Anthus pratensis*
Abundant winter visitor.

Red-throated Pipit *Anthus cervinus*
Passage migrant in very small numbers in April and October.

Water Pipit *Anthus spinoletta*
Breeds very sparingly at high altitude in the Sierra Nevada and possibly in Cazoria. Otherwise a common winter visitor to wetlands.

Yellow Wagtail *Motacilla flava*
Common migrant and local breeding resident of damp plains.

Grey Wagtail *Motacilla cinerea*
A conspicuous migrant, especially in October. Breeds by rocky streams and also winters in many places.

White Wagtail *Motacilla alba*
Abundant wintering species. Breeds in many areas, but sparingly.

Dipper *Cinclus cinclus*
Scarce and local on mountain streams.

Wren *Troglodytes troglodytes*
A resident of mainly mountain woodland, spreading to lower levels in winter.

Alpine Accentor *Prunella collaris*
Breeds at high levels in the Sierra Nevada, descending occasionally to coastal areas in winter.

Rufous Bush Robin *Cercotrichas galactotes*
Locally common but inconspicuous in scrub and plantations, arriving in late April.

Robin *Erythacus rubecula*
Resident locally and abundant winter visitor from the north.

Nightingale *Luscinia megarhynchos*
Summer visitor, often heard from damp entanglements anywhere.

Bluethroat *Luscinia svecica*
Common but retiring winter visitor to reedbeds and passage migrant.

Black Redstart *Phoenicurus ochruros*
Breeds in mountain areas. Abundant in winter, often in urban environments.

Redstart *Phoenicurus phoenicurus*
Summer resident of upland woods, but scarce and local. Common migrant on the coasts.

Whinchat *Saxicola rubetra*
Common passage migrant, usually in April and September.

Stonechat *Saxicola torquata*
A very common resident gracing practically every roadside.

Northern Wheatear *Oenanthe oenanthe*
Breeds on higher mountains in the region. Common on passage, sometimes appearing as late as December and as early as mid-February.

Black-eared Wheatear *Oenanthe hispanica*
Summer visitor to bare sunny hillsides and plains. Arrives a little later than the last species.

Black Wheatear *Oenanthe leucura*
Resident in rocky areas both on mountains and along coasts.

Rock Thrush *Monticola saxatilis*
Local summer visitor to rocky areas at high levels.

Blue Rock Thrush *Monticola solitarius*
Resident of rocky areas at low levels, taking readily to man-made structures.

Ring Ouzel *Turdus torquatus*
Winter visitor when flocks may be found in high valleys and passage migrant.

Blackbird *Turdus merula*
Common resident.

Song Thrush *Turdus philomelus*
Common migrant and winter visitor.

Redwing *Turdus iliacus*
Regular nocturnal migrant, partricularly in October and winter visitor to wooded valleys.

Mistle Thrush *Turdus viscivorus*
Common breeding resident in woodland, often in mountain areas.

Cetti's Warbler *Cettia cetti*
Common resident of waterside vegetation.

Fan-tailed Warbler *Cisticola juncidis*
Common resident of grasslands and crops. Difficult not to hear in any lowland situation in the breeding season.

Grasshopper Warbler *Locustella naevia*
Fairly common passage bird on both journeys.

Savi's Warbler *Locustella luscinioides*
Nests along Guadalquivir valley and possibly in Almería and Murcia, arriving in March.

Moustached Warbler *Acrocephalus melanopogon*
Scarce resident of reedbeds in Almería and Murcia.

Sedge Warbler *Acrocephalus melanopogon*
Fairly common passage migrant.

Reed Warbler *Acrocephalus scirpaceus*
Breeds in reedbeds throughout.

Great Reed Warbler *Acrocephalus arundinaceus*
Possibly more numerous than previous species and found in almost any reedbed throughout the region.

Olivaceous Warbler *Hippolais pallida*
A rare summer visitor to scrub and tamarisk, often in semi-desert, and possibly Murcia.

Melodious Warbler *Hippolais polyglotta*
Breeds in entanglements, sometimes by water, throughout the region showing a preference for higher altitudes.

Dartford Warbler *Sylvia undata*
A local resident of upland scrub descending to become an abundant wintering species in coastal parks and gardens.

Spectacled Warbler *Sylvia conspicillata*
Breeds in very low scrub, in salt flats and semi-desert, some birds overwintering.

Subalpine Warbler *Sylvia cantillans*
Breeds at the margins of montane woodland. Common on passage on the coast, often arriving early in March.

Sardinian Warbler *Sylvia melanocephalus*
Resident of parks, gardens, olive groves and scrub. Very common, often wintering in reedbeds with other species.

Orphean Warbler *Sylvia hortensis*
Not uncommon in mature woodland, from coastal pines to upland oak woods, a latish summer visitor, often still on passage in mid-May.

Whitethroat *Sylvia communis*
Scarce upland breeding species in scrub. Common coastal migrant.

Garden Warbler *Sylvia borin*
Local breeding bird in western parts. Common on passage.

Blackcap *Sylvia atricapilla*
Resident in some areas, notably around Granada. Abundant in winter anywhere.

Bonelli's Warbler *Phylloscopus bonelli*
Summer visitor to upland woods, breeding up to the tree line.

Wood Warbler *Phylloscopus sibilatrix*
Scarce but regular migrant.

Chiffchaff *Phylloscopus collybita*
Local breeding bird, passage migrant and enormously abundant wintering species, especially in reedbeds.

Willow Warbler *Phylloscopus trochilus*
Common passage migrant.

Firecrest *Phylloscopus trochilus*
The only resident species in this genus, found mainly in coniferous woods.

Spotted Flycatcher *Musicapa striata*
Common summer visitor.

Pied Flycatcher *Ficedula hypoleuca*
Common migrant and occasional breeding species, normally in riverine woods.

Bearded Tit *Panurus biarmicus*
Unpredictable visitor to reedbeds in the region. Probably does not breed.

Long-tailed Tit *Aegithalos caudatus*
Locally common species of woodland, often at higher altitudes, wandering typically in winter.

Crested Tit *Parus cristatus*
Most common in coniferous woodland, but also found in deciduous trees. Found throughout the region.

Coal Tit *Parus ater*
Widespread resident of mountain pine woods.

Blue Tit *Parus caeruleus*
Common resident of woodland, absent from southeastern coastal areas in Murcia Province, restricted to higher mountain sites.

Great Tit *Parus major*
Common resident, occupying a wide variety of habitats at all altitudes.

Nuthatch *Siita Europea*
A scarce and local resident of dehesa and cork-oak woodland. Absent from Murcia.

Short-toed Treecreeper *Certhia brachydactyla*
Widespread but rather local with a preference for mature pine woods, usually montane. Wanders, often to coastal locations, outside the breeding season. The Treecreeper *C. familiaris* is not recorded from the region and can practically be discounted.

Penduline Tit *Remiz pendulinis*
Breeds sparingly and locally, most usually in the valley of the Guadalquivir, when it may be found in reedbeds, usually with attendant tamarisk or other bushes. Much more numerous in winter, though often shy and retiring.

Golden Oriole *Oriolus oriolus*
A summer visitor, arriving in late April and having a preference for poplar plantation in riverine sites. Also, however, found in any type of woodland, even up to altitudes of 1,000 metres or more.

Great Grey Shrike *Lanius excubitor*
A common resident of agricultural and natural open country as well as reedbeds, which it frequents in winter, when numbers are greatly increased.

Woodchat Shrike *Lanius senator*
Very common summer resident, arriving quite early in March and mostly departing by the end of September.

Jay *Garrulus glandarius*
Locally common in oak woodlands, often in the sierras.

Azure-winged Magpie *Cyanopica cyana*
The classic 'dehesa' species, abundant in such open woodland in northern Córdoba and Jaén Provinces, less so in coastal pines of Sevilla and Cádiz.

Magpie *Pica pica*
Common resident, absent from some coastal areas.

Chough *Pyrrhocorax pyrrhocorax*
The only resident species of this genus, found in rocky mountains, in fact wherever suitable cliffs or caves exist. Sizeable flocks may form in winter.

Jackdaw *Corvus monedula*
Common resident, often in towns and cities, but co-exists with the last species on many crags.

Carrion Crow *Corvus corone*
A scarce resident of the Sierra de Cazoria, the upland plains of Murcia and similar regions of Granada Province where they are locally common.

Raven *Corvus corax*
A numerous and widespread resident of all sierras, also found at sea level, especially around Doñana.

Starling *Sturnus vulgaris*
Big flocks occur in winter, often forming large noisy roosts in orchards and the like. Absent in the breeding season.

Spotless Starling *Sturnus unicolor*
A common resident of farms, villages and towns throughout. Does not normally flock to the extent of the previous species from which it tends to stay apart.

House Sparrow *Passer domesticus*
Abundant resident.

Spanish Sparrow *Passer hispaniolensis*
Local resident, to be found in flocks at field margins often in northern Córdoba and Sevilla. Totally absent from most other areas, through birds may well be met with during passage times. In some areas apparent hybrids with the last species occur, though the two species often nest in close proximity (occasionally both use the substructure of the same White Stork's nest) and seem to retain their specific integrity.

Tree Sparrow *Passer montanus*
A remarkably scarce bird. Quite numerous in one small area in western Almería, however, and scattered colonies may be found almost anywhere.

Rock Sparrow *Petronia petronia*
A very hard species to guarantee, with a seemingly catholic taste in habitats. Breeds normally in rocky gorges, but flocks may be found in widely varying places, from rocky ground outside little hamlets on a Murcian plain to a car park at the very top of the Sierra Nevada. Cliff faces, however, provide the best opportunities.

Common Waxbill *Estrilda astrild*
A feral species now established but very local in reedbeds where small groups of six or ten pairs may be found.

Avadavat *Amandava amandava*
As last species. Small colonies may appear almost anywhere, again usually in aquatic sites.

Chaffinch *Fringilla coelebs*
A common resident of woodlands, usually at higher altitudes. In winter large numbers appear from the north.

Brambling *Fringilla montifringilla*
A scarce winter visitor and passage migrant.

Serin *Serinus serinus*
A very numerous and widespread species, found in natural woodland of practically all types, as well as in cultivated fruit trees, particularly of citrus.

Citril Finch *Serinus citrinella*
A winter visitor to the highest sierras, which may well breed in very small numbers in the Sierra de Cazoria. To be looked for in tree-line pines.

Greenfinch *Carduelis chloris*
Abundant resident and passage migrant.

Goldfinch *Carduelis carduelis*
Like many finches, this species moves in response to food availability, but is present throughout the year and is to be found anywhere.

Siskin *Carduelis spinus*
Fairly common winter visitor to pine woods.

Linnet *Carduelis cannabina*
Common resident, winter visitor and passage migrant.

Crossbill *Loxia ocurvirostra*
Locally common breeding species, usually in mountain areas, though flocks may be seen in coastal areas in some years.

Trumpeter Finch *Bucanetes githagineus*
Small colonies of this North African species have become established in Almería and probably Murcia. Flocks and wanders in winter and passage times have seen individuals occuring at many widely-spaced sites.

Bullfinch *Pyrrhula pyrrhula*
A scarce but annual winter visitor.

Hawfinch *Coccothraustes cthraustes*
Found in quiet oak woodlands throughout, to be looked for when it indulges its notorious thirst.

Cirl Bunting *Emberiza cirlus*
Common resident of open wooded hills. Not normally found at lower levels.

Rock Bunting *Emberiza cia*
Common in pine woods at high altitudes, usually, though not always, on rocky ground.

Ortolan Bunting *Emberiza hortulans*
Regular passage migrant, usually in small numbers, in April and September.

Reed Bunting *Emberiza schoeniclus*
A scarce breeding species of some reedbeds and abundant winter visitor.

Corn Bunting *Miliaria calandra*
A characteristic species of open country, both cultivated and otherwise. Found throughout the region, though not so easily located in winter, when flocks wander away from their breeding areas.

Vagrants and Accidentals in the Region

A glance at the map will suffice to convince anyone that the potential for African over-shooting migrants and wandering rarities is considerable. There is also an excellent chance of Nearctic wanderers from across the Atlantic, windblown Siberian vagrants and wandering seabirds. In other words, the region is at an avian crossroads and birds from many points of origin can and do occur here.

A bland list of all records to date would be quite unhelpful in the context of what can be expected as it is entirely likely that the first major rarity you find will not have been recorded before.

Below, I have included a summary of the likely and possible candidates for vagrancy, together with a few of the feral forms not mentioned elsewhere by family.

Divers and Grebes

The rarer divers may well occur in winter, most likely on the Atlantic coast. There are records of Slavonian Grebe, but few and certainly not annually.

Tube-noses

The potential list here is long — virtually any Atlantic petrel can occur, especially after gales and there are a significant number of records of Little Shearwater. Bulwer's Petrel has been trapped to the north of the region in the Mediterranean in recent years and a sea trip well out off the Atlantic shores may well reveal much of interest.

Gannets

Difficulties of distinction from *S. bassana* probably prevent Cape Gannet *S. capensis* from being better recorded, but records are claimed from time to time. There have also been records of at least two species of Booby which species wander extensively in the Atlantic.

Herons and the like

Great White Egret is now occurring regularly just to the north of our region and is to be looked for, particularly in autumn and winter. Of the African species, many are candidates for vagrancy, none more so than the Reef Heron, which has turned up several times in the past.

Lesser Flamingo occasionally puts in an appearance in the company of its larger cousins. Captive origins are always probable in this case.

Wildfowl

Mute Swans appear along the coasts of Almería and Murcia from time to time and may well attempt to colonise in the future. Bewick's occurs a little way to the north and could well wander to their region. The Greylag Geese which winter in Doñana frequently bring along fellow travellers which can include virtually any Palearctic goose species. Most have already been recorded in ones and twos.

Duck provide a vast array of possibilities, including the now almost routine Nearctic vagrants, American Wigeon, Blue-wing Teal and Ring-necked Duck, all of which have been recorded from Cádiz and Doñana. Eider and Long-tailed Duck are amongst the sea-ducks most likely to be found, whilst Goldeneye may well accompany the many Pochard which occur annually.

Raptors

Spotted Eagle is a winter wanderer always likely at Andalucian wetlands, as it occurs with some frequency a little to the north. Long-legged Buzzard breeds almost within sight of the Spanish coast in Morocco and has occurred several times. Spring records of wind-drifted Red-footed Falcon are not unusual, whilst Lanner and Pallid Harrier show up very occasionally. Lemming years may well bring a Rough-legged Buzzard south of its usual range. Peregrines on southern coasts should always be scrutinised for the possibility of a Barbary Falcon.

Rails

Corncrake MUST pass through in small numbers. Its Spanish name means 'Guide of the Quails' — how do they find one another? Allen's Gallinule is a fairly frequent vagrant from Africa.

Waders

Dotterel pass quickly through and the American Golden Plover is something to be vigilant for.

Most of the 'standard' Nearctic Waders have been recorded a time or two, but less frequently than, for example, in Britain. This is probably nothing more than an indication of the lack of trained observers here and the sheer scale of the area. An indication of this was brought home when I took a group to Almería in the autumn of 1994 and the first bird we saw was a juvenile Terek Sandpiper, very close to the road and not recorded by anyone else! Imagine that happening in Britain! That species is clearly another candidate for vagrancy, as presumably, is Broad-billed Sandpiper, but THE Blue Riband bird would be a Slender-billed Curlew, which habitually winters — probably the entire world population — on a marsh in northern Morocco. There are winter records from the Coto Doñana: Hope springs eternal!

Gulls

The normal American wanderers have been recorded, Ring-billed Laughing and Franklin's Gulls. Iceland and other Arctic Gulls can occur and Sabine's is more-or-less regular at sea.

Terns

Roseate and Arctic Terns can accompany migrating Commons, Royal Tern is reputed to be practically annual in the Straits and various terns of the southern oceans are 'on the cards'.

Parakeets

Ring-necked and Monk Parakeets have both established isolated feral communities in the Málaga area and the latter also breed at the northern limits of Murcia. Odd birds may be met with anywhere.

Swifts

Although identification would be difficult, the possibility of a Plain Swift from Canarian breeding populations, should not be discounted. The African Little Swift is more likely, however, with a few records in existence.

Larks to Bulbuls

There are many species of lark endemic to North Africa and, although they are largely sedentary, it may be worth being on guard for wanderers. Shore Lark has been recorded.

Richard's Pipit has been recorded in winter from Doñana.

Common Bulbul has apparently bred, both in Granada and Cádiz Provinces, but little is known of the records.

Thrushes and Chats

A range of largely sedentary African Wheatears look good candidates for a guest appearance and there are records of Desert and White-crowned Black. Fieldfares turn up in some winters.

Warblers and Flycatchers

Blyth's Reed Warbler, Marsh Warbler and Aquatic Warbler have all been trapped in ringing programmes, but certainly all occur scarcely. Marmora's Warbler records are always regarded with some scepticism by the Spanish authorities, due to the real possibility of confusion with individuals of Dartford Warbler. There remains, however, the strong possibility of a 'good' one, at almost any point near the coast and probably at passage times. You will need familiarity with the species and particularly its calls.

All the Siberian warblers recorded in Britain must be possible and many have occurred. The possibility of a Desert Warbler or a Tristram's should not be forgotten.

Red-breasted and Collared Flycatchers have both been found in Doñana and elsewhere.

Creepers, Shrikes and Crows

Wallcreeper turns up very occasionally on rock faces in the winter; Red-backed Shrike is rarer than may be supposed and there are (very) old records of Masked Shrike from Doñana.

Alpine Chough is seen from time to time at Gibraltar and in the mountains.

Finches

Someone of questionable sanity released Red-billed Quelea in Doñana, but they do not appear to have flourished. Scarlet Rosefinch is an occasional vagrant in Doñana.

Buntings

The Siberian buntings are all possibilities, especially in autumn. To date, there are records of Pine, Rustic and Little, amongst those likely to be of wild origin.

Snow Bunting and Yellowhammer are two northern species which have wandered this far south.

There are as yet few records of American passerines and we are, of course, well to the south of the main 'storm-track', but the possibility of birds crossing the Atlantic further north in the autumn then heading south to occur here should be considered a possible scenario.

Records of the above and other interesting species will be well received by:
Dr Eduardo de Juana,
Comite Iberico de Rarezas,
SEO,
Facultad de Biología, planta 9,
Cuidad Universitaria,
28040 Madrid.
You can write, if you prefer, in English.

Rapid Guide to 'key' Species

This chapter is designed to help those who may never have visited the region before, who have a limited time at their disposal and wish to plan a 'lightning raid', taking in the maximum possible number of 'key' species — i.e. those which they are quite unlikely to see elsewhere — the Southern Iberian Specialities. The list is necessarily subjective and the site(s) indicated for each species is selected on the basis of being, in the author's view, the best chance of seeing that species, for the minimum expenditure of time. Column two indicates the recommended site, in MOST YEARS. Column three, your chances of seeing the species on a visit of four hours' duration. Column four, the best time of year. It may be noted that birds, being unable to read well, may have differing opinions:

Species	Recommended site(s)	/10	Season
Little Bittern	Doñana, Cañada de las Norias	10	Summer
Night Heron	Córdoba	10	Spring
Cattle Egret	Córdoba, Doñana, etc	10	Any
Squacco Heron	Doñana, Lagunas de Terry	6	Summer
Black Stork	Sierras de Hornachuelos & Morena	5	Spring
Spoonbill	Doñana, Odiel (Huelva)	8	Summer
Marbled Duck	Doñana, Cañada de las Norias	5	Spr/Aut
Ferruginous Duck	Laguna de Medina	1	Winter
White-headed Duck	Adra, Cañada de las Norias	10	Any
Black-shouldered Kite	Doñana, N. Córdoba	7	Any
Griffon Vulture	Doñana, Tarifa, Cazorla	10	Any
Black Vulture	Andújar, Morena	9	Any
Short-toed Eagle	Cazorla, Andújar, Teba, etc	9	Spring
Montagu's Harrier	N. Córdoba, Carmona, etc	10	Spring
Goshawk	Andújar	3	Any
Imperial Eagle	Doñana, Andújar, Morena	2	Any
Bonelli's Eagle	Teba, Cazorla	6	Any
Lesser Kestrel	Towns and cities of western part	10*	Summer
Andalusian Hemipode	?	0	?
Purple Gallinule	Guadalquivir Reservoirs, L. de Zóñar	8	Spring
Crested Coot	Lagunas de Terry & Espera, Doñana	2	Any
Great Bustard	N. Córdoba	4	Winter
Little Bustard	Hoya de Guadix, Níjar, Alcanara	7	Win/Spr
Collared Pratincole	Doñana, Algaida, lagunas de Terry	9	Summer
Slender-billed Gull	Fuente de Piedra	4	Spring
Audouin's Gull	Salinas de Cabo de Gata, Adra	10	Any
Gull-billed Tern	Fuente de Piedra, Doñana, Algaida	6	Spring
Black-b Sandgrouse	Alcanara, H. de Guadix, Níjar	8	Any
Pin-tailed Sandgrouse	Doñana, Algaida	3	Any
Great Spotted Cuckoo	Alcanara, N. Córdoba	6	Spring
Scops Owl	Towns with parks	8*+	Spring
Eagle Owl	Cazorla, Hornachuelos, Tarifa	2+	Win/Spr
Red-necked Nightjar	Doñana, Andújar, etc	5+	Summer
Pallid Swift	Mar Menor, Tarifa, etc	10	Spr/Aut
White-rumped Swift	Tarifa (Sierras), etc	4	Summer
Bee-Eater	Almost anywhere	10	Spr/Sum
Roller	Alcanara, N. Córdoba, etc	8	Spr/Sum
Dupont's Lark	Níjar, España, Hoya de Guadix	5+	Spring
Calandra Lark	Alcanara, N. Córdoba, La Janda, etc	10	Spring
Lesser Short-toed Lark	Alcanara, Almería coast, L. de Terry	9	Any

Species	Recommended site(s)	/10	Season
Thekla Lark	Almost any sierra	10	Any
Red-rumped Swallow	Andújar, N. Córdoba, Tarifa sierras	10	Summer
Alpine Accentor	Sierra Nevada	9	Any
Rufous Bush Robin	Níjar, Tabernas, Doñana	7	Summer
Bluethroat	Any reedbed of the region	2	Winter
Black-eared Wheatear	Mar Menor, Alcanara, Teba, etc	10	Spring
Black Wheatear	Cabo de Gata, Teba, etc	10	Any
Rock Thrush	S. Nevada, Cazorla	3	Summer
Blue Rock Thrush	Cabo de Gata, Espuña, Teba, etc	10	Any
Olivaceous Warbler	Níjar, etc	2	Summer
Spectacled Warbler	Alcanara, Níjar, Cabo de Gata	6	Spring
Orphean Warbler	Doñana, Algaida, etc	6	Summer
Bonelli's Warbler	Andújar, Cazorla	10	Spring
Crested Tit	Any mountain woods	10	Any
Woodchat Shrike	Anywhere	10	Summer
Azure-winged Magpie	Andújar	10	Any
Chough	Teba, Cazorla	10	Any
Spotless Starling	Anywhere	10	Any
Spanish Sparrow	N. Córdoba	7	Spring
Citril Finch	Cazorla	7	Spring
Trumpeter Finch	Níjar, Tabernas, Gata	3	Win/Spr
Rock Bunting	Cazora, Espúna, etc	10	Any

* — If you choose the right town! Try Estepa for Lesser Kestrel
+ — If you go out at the right hour of day!

Lesser Kestrel

Southern Spain Checklist

R = Resident   **S** = Summer   **W** = Winter
M= Migrant   **V** = Vagrant   **P** = Passage

					English name	Scientific name	Status
					Red-throated Diver	*Gavia stellata*	**W**
					Black-throated Diver	*Gavia arctica*	**V**
					Great Northern Diver	*Gavia immer*	**V**
					Little Grebe	*Tachybaptus ruficollis*	**RW**
					Great Crested Grebe	*Podiceps cristatus*	**RW**
					Slavonian Grebe	*Podiceps auritus*	**V**
					Black-necked Grebe	*Podiceps nigricollis*	**RW**
					Fulmar	*Fulmarus glacialis*	**V**
					Bulwer's Petrel	*Bulweria bulwerii*	**V**
					Cory's Shearwater	*Calonectris diomedea*	**P**
					Great Shearwater	*Puffinus gravis*	**V**
					Sooty Shearwater	*Puffinus griseus*	**V**
					Mediterranean Shearwater	*Puffinus yelkouan*	**R**
					Little Shearwater	*Puffinus assimilis*	**V**
					Wilson's Storm-Petrel	*Oceanites oceanicus*	**V**
					White-faced Storm-petrel	*Pelagodroma marina*	**V**
					European Storm-petrel	*Hydrobates pelagicus*	**R**
					Leach's Storm-petrel	*Oceanodroma leucorhoa*	**V**
					Madeiran Storm-petrel	*Oceanodroma castro*	**V**
					Masked Booby	*Sula dactylatra*	**V**
					Brown Booby	*Sula leucogaster*	**V**
					Northern Gannet	*Morus bassana*	**R**
					Cape Gannet	*Morus capensis*	**V**
					Great Cormorant	*Phalacrocorax carbo*	**W**
					Shag	*Phalacrocorax aristotelis*	**R?V**
					Great Bittern	*Botaurus stellaris*	**W**
					Little Bittern	*Ixobrychus minutus*	**S**
					Night Heron	*Nyctricorax nycticorax*	**SP**
					Squacco Heron	*Ardeola ralloides*	**S**
					Cattle Egret	*Bubulcus ibis*	**R**
					Western Reef Heron	*Egretta gularis*	**V**
					Little Egret	*Egretta garzetta*	**RSW**
					Great White Egret	*Egretta alba*	**W**
					Grey Heron	*Ardea cinerea*	**RW**
					Purple Heron	*Ardea purpurea*	**S**
					Black Stork	*Ciconia nigra*	**S**
					White Stork	*Ciconia ciconia*	**SP**
					Glossy Ibis	*Plegadis falcinellus*	**W**
					Eurasian Spoonbill	*Platalea leucorodia*	**R**
					Greater Flamingo	*Phoenicopterus ruber*	**R**
					Lesser Flamingo	*Phoenicopterus minor*	**V**
					Mute Swan	*Cygnus olor*	**V**
					Bewick's Swan	*Cygnus columbians*	**V**
					Bean Goose	*Anser fabalis*	**V**
					White-fronted Goose	*Anser albifrons*	**V**
					Greylag Goose	*Anser anser*	**W**

English name	Scientific name	Status
Snow Goose	*Anser caerulescens*	F
Barnacle Goose	*Branta leucopsis*	V
Brent Goose	*Branta bernicla*	V
Red-breasted Goose	*Branta ruficollis*	V
Ruddy Shelduck	*Tadorna ferruginea*	V
Common Shelduck	*Tadorna tadorna*	W
Eurasian Wigeon	*Anas penelope*	W
American Wigeon	*Anas americana*	V
Gadwall	*Anas strepera*	R
Common Teal	*Anas crecca*	W
Mallard	*Anas platyrhynchos*	RW
Northern Pintail	*Anas acuta*	W
Garganey	*Anas querquedula*	P
Blue-winged Teal	*Anas discors*	V
Northern Shoveler	*Anas clypeata*	RW
Marbled Duck	*Marmaronetta angustirostris*	R
Red-crested Pochard	*Netta rufina*	RW
Common Pochard	*Aythya ferina*	R
Ring-necked Duck	*Aythya collaris*	V
Ferruginous Duck	*Aythya nyroca*	R
Tufted Duck	*Aythya fuligula*	W
Eider	*Somateria mollissima*	V
Long-tailed Duck	*Clangula hyemalis*	V
Common Scoter	*Melanitta nigra*	W
Velvet Scoter	*Melanitta fusca*	V
Common Goldeneye	*Bucephala clangula*	V
Red-breasted Merganser	*Mergus serrator*	W
Ruddy Duck	*Oxyura jamaicensis*	V
White-headed Duck	*Oxyura leucocephala*	R
Honey-buzzard	*Pernis apivorus*	RP
Black-shouldered Kite	*Elanus caeeruleus*	R
Black Kite	*Milvus migrans*	R
Red Kite	*Milvus milvus*	R
Lammergeier	*Gypaetus barbatus*	R
Egyptian Vulture	*Neophron percnopterus*	RP
Griffon Vulture	*Fyps fulvus*	R
Monk Vulture	*Aegypius monachus*	R
Short-toed Eagle	*Circaetus gallicus*	SP
Marsh Harrier	*Circus aeruginosus*	RW
Hen Harrier	*Circus cyaneus*	W
Pallid Harrier	*Circus macrourus*	V
Montagu's Harrier	*Circus pygargus*	S
Northern Goshawk	*Accipiter nisus*	R
Eurasian Sparrowhawk	*Accipiter nisus*	R
Common Buzzard	*Buteo buteo*	R
Long-legged Buzzard	*Buteo ruginus*	V
Rough-legged Buzzard	*Buteo lagopus*	V
Spotted Eagle	*Aquila clanga*	W
Imperial Eagle	*Aquila heliaca*	R
Golden Eagle	*Aquila chrysaetos*	R
Booted Eagle	*Hieraaetus pennatus*	R

English name	Scientific name	Status
Bonelli's Eagle	*Hieraaetus fasciatus*	R
Osprey	*Pandion haliaetus*	PW
Lesser Kestrel	*Falco naumanni*	R
Common Kestrel	*Falco tinnunculus*	R
Red-footed Falcon	*Falco vespertinus*	V
Merlin	*Falco columbarius*	W
Hobby	*Falco subbuteo*	S
Lanner Falcon	*Falco biarmicus*	V
Peregrine Falcon	*Falco peregrinus*	R
Barbary Falcon	*Falco pelegrinoides*	V
Red-legged Partridge	*Alectoris rufa*	R
Quail	*Coturnix coturnix*	S
Common Pheasant	*Phasianus colchicus*	R
Water Rail	*Rallus aquaticus*	R
Spotted Crake	*Porzana porzana*	RP
Little Crake	*Porzana parva*	R
Baillon's Crake	*Porzana pusilla*	S
Corn Crake	*Crex crex*	P
Moorhen	*Gallinula chloropus*	R
Allen's Gallinule	*Porphyrula alleni*	V
Purple Swamp-hen	*Porphyrio porphyrio*	R
Common Coot	*Fulica atra*	R
Crested Coot	*Fulica cristata*	R
Common Coot	*Grus grus*	W
Little Bustard	*Tetrax tetrax*	R
Great Bustard	*Otis tarda*	R
Oystercatcher	*Haematopus ostralegus*	PW
Black-winged Stilt	*Himantopus himantopus*	R
Avocet	*Recurvirostra avosetta*	RW
Stone-curlew	*Burhinus oedicnemus*	R
Cream-coloured Courser	*Cursorius cursor*	V
Collared Pratincole	*Glareola pratincole*	S
Little Ringed Plover	*Charadrius dubius*	R
Great Ringed Plover	*Charadrius hiaticula*	PW
Kentish Plover	*Charadrius alexandrinus*	R
Dotterel	*Charadrius morinellus*	V
American Golden Plover	*Pluvialis dominica*	V
Golden Plover	*Pluvialis apricaria*	W
Grey Plover	*Pluvialis squatarola*	WP
Northern Lapwing	*Vanellus vanellus*	WR
Red Knot	*Calidris canutus*	PW
Sanderling	*Calidris alba*	PW
Little Stint	*Calidris minuta*	PW
Temminck's Stint	*Calidrus temminckii*	V
Curlew Sandpiper	*Calidris ferruginea*	PW
Purple Sandpiper	*Calidris maritima*	W
Dunlin	*Calidris alpina*	PW
Ruff	*Philomachus pugnax*	PW
Jack Snipe	*Lymnocryptes minimus*	W
Common Snipe	*Galinago galinago*	WP
Woodcock	*Scolopax rusticola*	W

84

English name	Scientific name	Status
Black-tailed Godwit	*Limosa limosa*	PW
Bar-tailed Godwit	*Limosa lapponica*	PW
Whimbrel	*Numenius phaeopus*	PW
Eurasian Curlew	*Numenius arquata*	PW
Spotted Redshank	*Tringa erythropus*	PW
Common Redshank	*Tringa totanus*	RW
Marsh Sandpiper	*Tringa stagnatilis*	PW
Common Redshank	*Tringa nebularia*	PW
Green Sandpiper	*Tringa ochropus*	PW
Terek Sandpiper	*Xenus cinerus*	V
Wood Sandpiper	*Tringa glareola*	PW
Common Sandpiper	*Actitis hypoleucos*	R
Turnstone	*Arenaria interpres*	P
Red-necked Phalarope	*Phalaropus lobatus*	P
Grey Phalarope	*Phalaropus fulicarius*	W
Pomarine Skua	*Stercorarius pomarinus*	P
Arctic Skua	*Stercorarius parasiticus*	PW
Great Skua	*Stercorarius skua*	PW
Mediterranean Gull	*Larus melanocephalus*	P
Laughing Gull	*Larus atrcilla*	V
Franklin's Gull	*Larus pipixcan*	V
Little Gull	*Larus minutus*	PW
Sabine's Gull	*Larus sabini*	V
Black-headed Gull	*Larus ridibundus*	PW
Slender-billed Gull	*Larus genei*	R
Audouin's Gull	*Larus audouinii*	P
Ring-billed Gull	*Larus delawarensis*	V
Lesser Black-backed Gull	*Larus fuscus*	W
Yellow-legged Gull	*Larus cachinnans*	R
Iceland Gull	*Larus glaucoides*	V
Kittiwake	*Rissa tridactyla*	V
Gull-billed Tern	*Gelochelidon nilotica*	S
Caspian Tern	*Sterna caspia*	PW
Royal Tern	*Sterna maxima*	V
Lesser Crested Tern	*Sterna bengalensis*	V
Sandwich Tern	*Sterna sandvicensis*	PW
Roseate Tern	*Sterna dougallii*	V
Common Tern	*Sterna hirundo*	P
Arctic Tern	*Sterna paradisaea*	V
Little Tern	*Sterna albifrons*	S
Whiskered Tern	*Chlidonias hybridus*	S
Black Tern	*Chlidonias niger*	S
White-winged Black Tern	*Chlidonias leucopterus*	P
Razorbill	*Alca torda*	PW
Puffin	*Fratercula arctica*	PW
Black-bellied Sandgrouse	*Pterocles orientalis*	R
Pin-tailed Sandgrouse	*Pterocles alchata*	R
Rock Dove	*Columa livia*	R
Stock Dove	*Columba oenas*	R
Wood Pigeon	*Columa palumbus*	R
Collared Dove	*Streptopelia decaocto*	R

English name	Scientific name	Status
Turtle Dove	*Streptopelia turtur*	SP
Great Spotted Cuckoo	*Clamator glandarius*	SP
Common Cuckoo	*Ciculus canorus*	SP
Ring-necked Parakeet	*Psittacula krameri*	F
Monk Parakeet	*Myopsitta monachus*	F
Barn Owl	*Tyto alba*	R
Eurasian Scops Owl	*Otus scops*	S
Eagle Owl	*Bubo bubo*	R
Little Owl	*Athene noctua*	R
Tawny Owl	*Strix aluco*	R
Long-eared Owl	*Asio otus*	R
Short-eared Owl	*Asio fammeus*	PW
European Nightjar	*Caprimulgus europaeus*	S
Red-necked Nightjar	*Caprimulgus ruficollis*	S
Common Swift	*Apus apus*	S
Pallid Swift	*Apus pallidus*	S
Alpine Swift	*Apus melba*	S
White-rumped Swift	*Apus caffer*	S
Little Swift	*Apusa affinis*	V
Common Kingfisher	*Alcedo atthis*	R
European Bee-eater	*Merops apiaster*	S
European Roller	*Coracias garrulus*	S
Hoopoe	*Upupa epops*	S
Wryneck	*Jynx torquilla*	R
Green Woodpecker	*Picus viridis*	R
Great Spotted Woodpecker	*Dendrocopos major*	R
Lesser Spotted Woodpecker	*Dendrocopos minor*	R
Dupont's Lark	*Chersophilus duponti*	R
Calandra Lark	*Melanocorypha calandra*	R
Shore Lark	*Eremophila alpestris*	V
Short-toed Lark	*Calandrella brachydactyla*	S
Lesser Short-toed Lark	*Calandrella rufescens*	R
Crested Lark	*Galerida cristata*	R
Thekla Lark	*Galerida theklae*	R
Wood Lark	*Lullula arborea*	R
Sky Lark	*Alauda arvensis*	WR
Sand Martin	*Riparia riparia*	S
Crag Martin	*Ptyonoprogne rupestris*	R
Barn Swallow	*Hirundo rustica*	SP
Red-rumped Swallow	*Hirundo daurica*	SP
House Martin	*Delichon urbica*	S
Richard's Pipit	*Anthus novaeseelandiae*	W
Tawny Pipit	*Anthus campestris*	SP
Tree Pipit	*Anthus trivialis*	P
Meadow Pipit	*Anthus pratenswis*	PW
Red-throated Pipit	*Anthus cervinus*	P
Water Pipit	*Anthus spinoletta*	WR
Yellow Wagtail	*Motacilla flava*	PR
Grey Wagtail	*Motacilla cinerea*	R
White Wagtail	*Motacilla alba*	PR
Garden Bulbul	*Pycnonotus barbatus*	R?

English name	Scientific name	Status
Dipper	*Cinclus cinclus*	R
Wren	*Troglodytes troglodytes*	R
Dunnock	*Prunella modularis*	P
Alpine Accentor	*Prunella collaris*	R
Rufous-tailed Scrub-robin	*Cercotrichas galactotes*	S
Robin	*Erithacus rubecula*	R
Rufous Nightingale	*Luscinia megarhynchos*	S
Bluethroat	*Luscinia svecica*	WP
Black Redstart	*Phoenicurus ochruros*	RPW
Common Redstart	*Phoenicurus*	SP
Whinchat	*Saxicola rubetra*	P
Common Stonechat	*Saxicola torquata*	R
Northern Wheatear	*Oenanthe oenanthe*	RP
Black-eared Wheatear	*Oenanthe hispanica*	SP
Desert Wheatear	*Oenanthe deserti*	V
White-crowned Black Wheatear	*Oenanthe leucopyga*	V
Black Wheatear	*Oenanthe leucura*	R
Rock Thrush	*Monticola saxatilis*	SP
Blue Rock Thrush	*Monticola solitarius*	R
Ring Ouzel	*Turdus torquatus*	PW
Blackbird	*Turdus merula*	R
Fieldfare	*Turdus pilaris*	W
Song Thrush	*Turdus philomelos*	PW
Redwing	*Turdus iliacus*	PW
Mistle Thrush	*Turdus viscivorus*	R
Cetti's Warbler	*Cettia cetti*	R
Zitting Cisticola	*Cisticola juncidis*	R
Grasshopper Warbler	*Locustella naevia*	P
Savi's Warbler	*Locustella luscinioides*	S
Moustached Warbler	*Acrocephalus melanopogon*	R
Aquatic Warbler	*Acrocephalus paludicola*	P
Sedge Warbler	*Acrocephalus schoenobaenus*	P
Marsh Warbler	*Acrocephalus palustris*	V
Reed Warbler	*Acrocephalus scirpaceus*	S
Great Reed Warbler	*Acrocephalus arundinaceus*	S
Livaceous Warbler	*Hippolais pallida*	S
Melodious Warbler	*Hippolais polyglotta*	S
Dartford Warbler	*Sylvia undata*	R
Spectacled Warbler	*Sylvia conspicillata*	R
Subalpine Warbler	*Sylvia cantillans*	PS
Sardinian Warbler	*Sylvia melanocephala*	R
Orphean Warbler	*Sylvia hortensis*	S
Whitethroat	*Sylvia communus*	SP
Garden Warbler	*Sylvia borin*	SP
Blackcap	*Sylvia atricapilla*	R
Radde's Warbler	*Phylloscopus schwarzi*	V
Bonelli's Warbler	*Phylloscopus bonelli*	S
Wood Warbler	*Phylloscopus sibilatrix*	P
Chiffchaff	*Phylloscopus collybia*	R
Willow Warbler	*Phylloscopus trochilus*	R
Goldcrest	*Regulus regulus*	V

English name	Scientific name	Status
Firecrest	*Regulus ignicapillus*	R
Spotted Flycatcher	*Muscicapa striata*	SP
Pied Flycatcher	*Ficedula hypoleuca*	SP
Collared Flycatcher	*Ficedula albicollis*	V
Red-breasted Flycatcher	*Ficedula parva*	V
Bearded Tit	*Panurus biarmicus*	V
Long-tailed Tit	*Aegithalos caudatus*	R
Crested Tit	*Parus cristatus*	R
Coal Tit	*Parus ater*	R
Blue Tit	*Parus caeruleus*	R
Great Tit	*Parus major*	R
Wood Nuthatch	*Sitta europaea*	R
Wallcreeper	*Tichodroma muraria*	W
Short-toed Treecreeper	*Carthia brachydactyla*	R
Penduline Tit	*Remiz pendulinus*	R
Golden Oriole	*Oriolus oriolus*	S
Red-backed Shrike	*Lanius collurio*	P
Great Grey Shrike	*Lanius excubitor*	R
Woodchat Shrike	*Lanius senator*	S
Masked Shrike	*Lanius nubicus*	V
Eurasian Jay	*Garrulus glandarius*	R
Magpie	*Pica pica*	R
Azure-winged Magpie	*Cyanopica cyana*	R
Yellow-billed Chough	*Pyrrhocorax graculus*	V
Red-billed Chough	*Pyrrhocorax pyrrhocorax*	R
Eurasian Jackdaw	*Corvus monedul*	R
Carrion Crow	*Corvus corone*	R
Common Raven	*Corvus corax*	R
Common Starling	*Sturnus vulgaris*	W
Spotless Starling	*Sturnus unicolor*	R
House Sparrow	*Passer domesticus*	R
Spanish Sparrow	*Passer hispaniolensis*	R
Tree Sparrow	*Passer montanus*	R
Rock Sparrow	*Petronia petronia*	R
Avadavat	*Amandava amandava*	F
Common Waxbill	*Estrida astrild*	F
Chaffinch	*Fringilla coelebs*	RPW
Brambling	*Fringilla montifringill*	PW
Citril Finch	*Serinus citrinella*	W
European Serin	*Serinus serinus*	R
Greenfinch	*Carduelis chloris*	R
Goldfinch	*Carduelis carduelis*	R
Siskin	*Carduelis spinus*	W
Linnete	*Acanthis cannabina*	RPW
Common Crossbill	*Loxia curvirostra*	R
Trumpeter Finch	*Bucanetes githagineus*	R
Common Rosefinch	*Carpodacus erythrinus*	V
Bullfinch	*Pyrrhula pyrrhula*	W
Hawfinch	*Coccothraustes coccothraustes*	R
Snow Bunting	*Plectophenax nivalis*	V
Corn Bunting	*Miliaria calandra*	RW

English name	Scientific name	Status
Pine Bunting	*Emberiza leucocephalus*	V
Rock Bunting	*Emberiza cia*	R
Little Bunting	*Emberiza pusilla*	V
Yellowhammer	*Emberiza citrinella*	V
Rustic Bunting	*Emberiza rustica*	V
Cirl Bunting	*Emberiza cirlus*	R
Ortolan Bunting	*Emberiza hortulana*	P
Reed Bunting	*Emberiza schoeniclus*	R

ACCIDENTALS

NOTES

NOTES